Preaching Doctrine

Preaching Doctrine

For the Twenty-First Century

Robert G. Hughes
and Robert Kysar

Fortress Press
Minneapolis

PREACHING DOCTRINE
For the Twenty-First Century

Cover and text designed by Joseph Bonyata.

Library of Congress Cataloging-in-Publication Data

Hughes, Robert G.
  Preaching doctrine : for the twenty-first century / Robert G.
 Hughes and Robert Kysar.
   p. cm. — (Fortress resources for preaching)
  Includes bibliographical references.
  ISBN 0-8006-2965-5 (alk. paper)
  1. Doctrinal preaching. I. Kysar, Robert. II. Title
III. Series
BV4235.D63H84 1997
251—dc21
                    97-23757
                      CIP

The paper used in this publication meets the minimum requirements of American Standard for Information Sciences—Permanence of Paper for Printed Library Materials, ANSI Z329.48-1984.

Manufactured in the U.S.A.   AF 1-2965

03 02 01 00 99 98 97 1 2 3 4 5 6 7 8 9 0

Contents

Acknowledgments

Teaching a subject is likely to force one to think more deeply about it. Therein lies the history of the origin of this book. In 1992 we decided to offer an elective senior-level course in preaching doctrine at the Lutheran Theological Seminary at Philadelphia (while Kysar was still a member of that faculty). As we searched for books to use in the course, we became aware of how little is available that directly addresses the issue. Much that had been written is now out of print or was written before the revolution that has been labeled the new homiletic. Because of the scarcity of recently published discussions of preaching theological themes, we decided that we would think about publishing the materials we were preparing for the course.

But it was not as easy as that. Our first offering of the course in the spring of 1993 was less than a wonderful success. Still, we wanted to learn from our experience, so we offered the course in a much revised version again the next spring. In the spring of 1996 each of us had the opportunity to teach the same or a comparable course at our current institutions, this time each paired with still another teacher.

This book is the result of the hard thinking forced on us by those teaching experiences. Not least of all, the content of each of the chapters was refined in the hot fires of our students' searching questions and insightful comments, as well as their puzzled expressions as we tried to expound a dimension of the subject. We were privileged to experience how many of our students took the material and improved on it in their own sermons for the course. Consequently, we acknowledge our deep debt to those some seventy-five students who indulged our early efforts to think systematically about preaching doctrine in a new century.

We must also acknowledge a good many others who have knowingly or unknowingly contributed to this volume. Our recent team teachers, namely, Pastor Christian Eichorn and Ms. Maisha Handy, each significantly influenced one of us. Obviously we stand indebted to a wide range of other scholars who are a part of the newest trends in homiletics, only some of whom are acknowledged in the notes. But we are grateful as well for a good many others whose work implicitly contributes to both the challenge and the possibilities of the sermon in the twenty-first century and especially to the role of theological formation in the congregation. Acknowledgment of indebtedness, however, does not transfer responsibility. We have used the work of others for our own purposes and cannot hold them responsible for what we have made of their good efforts.

Our thanks are due to our respective institutions as well. Hughes was granted a three-month sabbatical leave from his weighty responsibilities as president and professor of homiletics at the Lutheran Theological Seminary. That made it possible for him to find time once again to write—time he rarely has in his position. Kysar acknowledges the research and travel support Candler School of Theology affords him, which was of significant assistance in collaborating on this volume with Hughes while living some 750 miles to the south of him. That support also made possible a research assistant, the Reverend Ms. Nickie Stipe, whose careful proofreading vastly improved the quality of Kysar's contributions to this volume. Thanks go, as well and as always, to patient and supportive spouses who understand the importance of preaching and the theological formation of the laity but had to endure our moments of preoccupation with these pages.

Finally, we acknowledge all of the preachers who week after week enter the pulpit to speak a living Word for their congregations. Those of us who teach preaching recognize that thinking, speaking, and writing about it are far different from doing it on a weekly basis. This book is an expression of our deep appreciation of all the servants of the Word. Our prayer for this slender volume is that it might contribute in some useful way to their ministries, in whose debt we stand.

1

The Advent of a New Century

A child had been baptized at the Sunday morning service. After the service a woman approached the pastor in the narthex, obviously upset. A lifelong Lutheran and a faithful member of the congregation who attended worship with some regularity, she was rarely active in other congregational programs.

She challenged her pastor: "What was this I heard about priests in the baptism?" He immediately assumed she had in mind the sentence in the baptismal service that reads, "Through Baptism God has made this new sister/brother a member of the priesthood we all share in Christ Jesus. . . ." (*Lutheran Book of Worship*, p. 124).

"We don't have priests!" she protested. "The Catholics—they have priests. But we don't! So, what was this about priests?"

There in the narthex, with congregants waiting to speak with him, the frustrated pastor tried to give the woman a sixty-second summary of the doctrine of the priesthood of all believers. But she was in no mood to hear or to learn doctrine on the spot. She walked away, still angry, muttering something about Catholics.

Nearly every pastor could relate an experience like this one. Something has radically changed. No longer can we assume that our congregation knows the tradition of its denomination. No longer can we take for granted a fundamental understanding of the basics of the faith. Something like a doctrinal defoliation has occurred. The rich doctrinal foliage of the contemporary church seems infested with a deadly disease. Something has radically changed. Something new is at work in our culture.

Any consideration of preaching in the twenty-first century must begin with asking what is new about the new century? Especially if we want to understand how clergy might renew their preaching of the classic doctrines of the church, we will need to make some preliminary observations about what has been gradually shaping us and those to whom we preach at the close of this century and the approaching advent of a new one. Preaching is a cultural event that always entails insights into how culture shapes the lives of both the preacher and the congregation.

In this introductory chapter we hope to weave together three discrete dimensions of the task of preaching doctrine in a new century. First, we will discuss some of the reasons for the gradual disintegration of theological sophistication among the laity. But that will lead us, second, into some analysis of the cultural movements that are discernible in the closing decades of the twentieth century. Finally, we will venture some suggestions as to the nature of theological reflection in the new century that is upon us.

The Demise of Theological Acumen

Many pastors are keenly aware of the creeping theological illiteracy abroad in most congregations today and have reaped some of its results. Perhaps many share that pastor's incomprehension of the woman's objection to the baptismal ritual. Along with an increasing biblical illiteracy among the laity, there is (not coincidentally) an equally disturbing spread of theological ignorance. A deadly disease is at work in many of the mainline Protestant churches of America—a disease that has afflicted us so quietly and subtly that it has become malignant without detection. What has brought on this malignancy?[1]

The Church's Responsibility

To ask about the demise of theological acumen unavoidably leads us into the swamp of cultural change. But, first, let the church and its ministry take their own share of responsibility for the situation. For numerous reasons, we are failing to educate people in the faith. In some cases confirmation courses have been watered down, and some leaders seriously question the whole practice of catechetical preparation—at least in terms of its doctrinal content. Adult education is often slighted, or has been so grossly unsuccessful that it has been minimized. The older adult Bible study during Sunday school may be the only surviving fragment of a congregation's adult education program. Other more popular issues, entertainment, and the desire to help people feel good elbow their way into prominence at the expense of teaching theology. In some cases clergy and other church leaders themselves have come to think that theological reflection is of secondary importance. Amid the pressures of parish ministry, the more practical issues of evangelism, stewardship, and church administration have risen to top priority. Hence, there is a kind of clerical anti-intellectualism abroad, with the result that theology is far less important than our seminary training made it. (Whose books sell the best among North American clergy, Jürgen Moltmann or Lyle Schaller?)

Contemporary preaching, too, cannot escape an allowance of blame, for it has contributed more than its share of theological superficiality. The demise of the three-point propositional linear sermon has had some unfortunate (and unintended) consequences. Attention may too often focus exclusively on personal or social issues, without articulation of the prerequisite doctrines underlying them. Stories may be told for their own sake, without attention to or even concern for the theological implications they carry. Sermons have been shortened to accommodate the listeners' shrinking attention span, and hence sustained arguments are nearly impossible. Teaching sound theology in preaching seems to have gone the way of the Edsel.

Culture's Responsibility

But the church itself has been the victim of broader cultural changes. We need a lengthier analysis of those changes in order to understand the emergence of an increasingly unschooled laity. Various factors have moved the church away from the centrality of its theological affirmations in the waning years of the twentieth century.

The first of these is that the church has increasingly become another of the victims of North American consumerism. In many parts of our nation, at least, people often choose their congregation much like they choose a new car. Denominational loyalty figures very little in their decision. Much more important are practical concerns, such as location and programs. The consequence of this consumerism is that in many congregations no single doctrinal basis, no common heritage of theology, prevails to unify parishioners. Pair this cultural phenomenon with the withering of new member education (and the priority placed on church growth), and you have the makings for theological confusion and doctrinal ignorance.

The second ingredient in this mixture is the radical individualism of today's church member. Parishioners often tend to view doctrinal beliefs as a matter of personal and private preference. There may even be a feeling that what I believe is no one's business but my own. Not even the pastor has the right to tell me what I should believe to be a Lutheran, a United Methodist, or whatever. So, at least some congregations appear to be hodgepodges of belief and are content to remain so. The community quality of congregations is less and less shared theological perspective and is reduced to what has been called "enclaves of like-mindedness."[2]

Third, in the cultural air we have breathed in the last third of the twentieth century, there seems to be an unquenchable desire for the simplistic—a craving for simple answers and easy solutions. The desire is nurtured among other things by the popular thirty-minute television drama format in which plots are always resolved naïvely and quickly. Fast foods and microwave ovens have made us want fast answers. Surely the marvelous pain-relief medicines that pride themselves on how quickly they work have played their part. The thirst also appears to be nurtured by a general quick-fix mentality. Any casual observer of the political climate at the end of the twentieth century in the United States sees that mentality applied to social problems in our nation. Our culture seems entranced by simplicity.

Hence, the simpler the religious faith, the better. Maybe the quest for the simplistic is due in part to the fact that many of us find life far too complicated as it is. We want our religion to be simple and to provide an escape from the complexities of life. This insistence on the simplistic deafens some people to theological discussion, for theology always sounds complicated. Many of us do not want an involved system of belief. Please, no paradox, no subtleties.

Part of the quest for simplicity involves the issue of authority. With traditional societal forms of authority crumbling all around us (for example, the family, the school, law enforcement), many North Americans search for an absolute, unquestionable authority. From such authority they gain simple answers to life's most complex questions. In some of the fastest-growing churches, the belief system advocated is the epitome of the simple, with absolute authority posited in the Bible alone, and by inference in the clergy who expound it. On the other hand, churches in which authority is admittedly far more ambiguous find it difficult to appeal to the general population.

A fourth factor contributing to the demise of a theologically educated laity is the cultural hesitancy to deal with—even the tendency to be suspicious of—concepts and abstractions. This tendency is evident, but its reasons complex. Has television, with its instantaneous images, diminished the capacity to conceptualize? You do not have to create an image in your mind, as the old radio dramas used to require; television provides it. Another influence has surely been the kind of literature that has become popular. Book sales are at a record high, but the books that sell seldom require conceptualization and abstraction. A possible result of these social tendencies is that many may feel intellectually inadequate and intimidated by theological issues. We do not understand how our electronic gadgets work. We cannot even program our VCRs. So how could we understand a complex doctrine? Some may feel they are not equipped to deal with the intricacies of abstract, logical, systematic thought and are threatened by such discussions.

But those of us in the church have too often been given to understand and teach that doctrine has to do with abstractions, conceptualization, and theoretical ideas. It has no basis in real, daily experience and is just a mind game that the gifted play. Somehow many of us have forgotten or failed to communicate that theology is always rooted in real visceral Christian experience. Insofar as the church—these writers and readers included—has cultivated that view of doctrine, we are again culpable for the theological cancer that resides among us.

A final cultural trend may aid the spread of this theological deformation, namely, the death of tradition. All around us there is a sense that the new slays the relevance of the old. And that has been true of many of the revolutions at the conclusion of the twentieth century, for instance, changes in the traditional family structure. But doctrine is part of our tradition as a Christian people. Our faith stands on the shoulders of countless Christian communities before us, and it is impossible to speak of theology without invoking its articulation in earlier centuries. Yet such talk sounds anachronistic to many a contemporary ear, like a discussion of smoke signals in a day of fax machines, electronic mail, and the Internet.

In summary, each of these factors (among others) has played a role in the demise of theological interest among the laity. Moreover, taken together they suggest the difficult task of enlivening traditional Christian doctrine even among some of the most devout and point toward the need for preaching to renew its commitment to theological formation. In many of our congregations today the sole opportunity for nurturing lay theological understanding is increasingly found in the

Sunday morning service of worship. Liturgy and hymnody play indispensable roles in that process.[3] But so too preaching provides us with rare teaching moments (see chapter 5). Preaching doctrine in a new century will need to take new forms because of wider cultural movements that have influenced all of us.

Wider Cultural Movements

Therefore, we should add to the trends mentioned above acknowledgment of three broader cultural currents witnessed in the last decades. Placed in their chronological order, they demonstrate the changing times in which we live and a direction important for any effort at the theological formation of Christian community.

The Radical Secularization of Culture

Modernism still nurtures secularization. While the secular city[4] was never fully actualized, secularization remains a helpful category in understanding what has transpired among us. Reality is still commonly understood as flat and one dimensional, desacralized and demystified of transcendent powers. We continue to operate daily on the assumption that the world is self-contained and explainable within itself. A popular pseudo-scientific presumption leads us to think that everything is the result of observable phenomena. We are even urged to buy our toothpaste on the basis of scientific data. Transcendence—another realm beyond the observable—seems at once either unnecessary or unfathomable. So, some are content to ignore any possibility beyond the empirical. Television, along with other media, persistently ingrains this perspective in popular mentality.[5]

Intellectually, secularism provides no framework within which the sermon's listeners can integrate references to a transcendent reality. God-talk usually necessitates that our listeners separate their churchly lives from the real, secular world in which they spend the vast majority of their time. The church and its preachers have, in some cases, tried to accommodate secularization. Sometimes we have had some degree of success in doing so. But often such efforts have led to a domesticated Christianity within secularism at the expense of the integrity of the gospel.

The domestication of Christianity takes at least two very different forms. It is witnessed in the revival of authoritarian fundamentalism, which persists in its steadfast claim that Christianity is empirically true.

We suspect that this form of Christian life and faith is actually a popular expression of modernism. Having fought and won (so they say) the battle with modernism, the result is a Christian thought that proves itself on secular terms (for example, the Bible proves the historical reality of Jesus' bodily resurrection). In this case, theological formation takes a peculiar form, namely, of indoctrination with the fundamentals of the biblical faith construed in terms of historical fact.

The other form of domestication may be found in a cultural Christianity that reinterprets the tradition in ways that are palatable to modernism. The psychologizing of the Christian message, for instance, concentrates on categories that are harmonious with the secular mentality, for example, a success Christianity that yields peace of mind and sometimes even material success. Self-fulfillment is enthroned as the eminent goal of religious faith. Implicit in this movement is the conviction that theology is not really important at all. It is not a matter of doctrinal clarity but of self-actualization.

The Emergence of a New Spirituality

Amid the radical secularization of our culture a revival of fascination with the spiritual has arisen.[6] This new spirituality appears to be a revolt against secularization's elimination of transcendence. It is sometimes a cry for help from those who feel trapped in the secular one-dimensional world and at times takes the form of a quest for the spiritual precisely because the secularized mind cannot accommodate transcendence. Some forms of the new spirituality of our culture seem even to be openly anti-intellectual, perhaps because the intellect of its advocates is still thoroughly secularized.

This antithetical movement has surfaced in nubilous forms in the last decades, some explicitly religious, some quasi-religious. In its least religious form, the quest for a spirituality is seen in a popular and sentimental creation of idols out of love and friendship.[7] Sometimes a fatalism is expressed which may or may not be related to traditional religions. But such fatalisms seem to acknowledge unknown and unfathomable transcendent forces over which the individual has no control (for example, I will die when my time has come). Self-help and New Age are still two other movements that suggest the thirst of the human spirit for something more beyond the world of natural cause and effect.

This new spirituality is present, too, in Christian forms or forms closer to traditional Christianity. Two of the most interesting are the sudden revival of the popularity of chant and angels. Both appear designed to renew an experience of a transcendent dimension in a flat world without depth. Angels have traditionally become important among Christians when God seemed remote and unreachable. Angels serve as mediators of the transcendent in place of the divine being.

Those of us who are leaders in the church hear again and again the cries of the rebels against secularism for something spiritual. What exactly we hear in those cries is not always clear, but the pleas are being answered with new attention to prayer, disciplined meditation, relationships, and community, among other things. Seminaries are creating new courses in spirituality or taking old ones out of curricular cold storage. Pastors are seeking graduate programs and continuing education in what has traditionally been labeled spirituality. It is clear that the clergy as well as the laity are caught up in this revival of spirituality.

Our concern is not to issue a judgment on this renewed interest in the spiritual. Indeed, in some cases it clearly signals a rebirth of Christianity. But we only suggest it be understood within its cultural context. We contend that the emergence of this new spirituality is directly related to secularism and the vacuum left by the shrinkage of biblical and theological understanding. On a popular level the new spirituality is sometimes being substituted where biblical literacy and doctrinal clarity once functioned in Christian life. Theology has too often become unrelated to life, and the spiritual quest seeks a renewal of the relevance of Christian faith. Indeed, some forms of the emerging new interest in spirituality are strong in theological substance, not least of all among feminist writers.[8] We shall try to show that nurturing theological reflection through preaching will affect that void so often called spiritual. But such doctrinal preaching will need to take some new forms, as we will suggest below.

The Birth of Postmodernism

The third wider cultural movement is far more clouded and uncertain. Cultural analysts, for the most part, seem to agree that the revolution of the final third of the twentieth century is so radical as to signal the end of the era of modernism and the beginning of a new age in North American culture. The title *postmodernism* is an empty and temporary tag we use for what we do not yet know. It denotes only the cultural spirit that succeeds modernism. The more specific nature of that new spirit cannot yet be named because it is still in formation and its maturation lies in the future. We use the expression here in the role of a temporary designation but also in the conviction that something new is being born among us.[9]

The premise of postmodern analysis is that the essential components of modernism are proving themselves inadequate and obsolete. The very foundations of the age, as we have known it, are crumbling. Indeed, it may be that the emergence of the new spirituality that challenges secularization may be one of the clearest indications of the changing times. Modernity's banishment of transcendence may be reversed in a postmodern world, but no one doubts that transcendence will return from its exile dressed in new garments.[10]

Clearly what is emerging, however, is more. When compared with modernism, postmodernism is minimally a new human consciousness, a new appreciation of the role of language and its social qualities, a suspicion of so-called universal truths, and a new understanding of human relationships. Science and technology will assume important roles in the new era—that no one can seriously doubt. But no longer will they serve as surrogate saviors, for the house within which the sciences lived for centuries has suffered radical renovation. Postmodernism for the present and near future will deconstruct much of what our culture has taken for granted. But its primary feature, we suggest, will not be nihilistic as may often now appear to be the case. Still, its reformation will reach far back into our cherished tradition to disengage us from much that took shape in the Enlightenment and succeeding decades.

There is, then, both a threat and an opportunity in the advent of a postmodern era in America. Postmodernism will be no easier on traditional Christianity than was modernism at its advent. It will work against any invoking of the past as the answer to the present. But it will stir in us all a new quest for an understanding of human existence that is sustainable in the contemporary situation. If Christianity can respond to that quest in authentic ways, we have the opportunity not only to survive but even flourish in the postmodern age in a more authentic way, that is, not merely as a cultural phenomenon, but as the gospel expressed in a new time.[11] Postmodernism deconstructs our stories—individual and social. Christianity has the opportunity to retell a story that fills the void of a storyless people.

Conclusion

The facts that have contributed to the demise of theological acumen need to be understood in the context of these wider cultural changes.

Seen in that larger context, they become simply a few of the threads in the whole fabric of our cultural history. Furthermore, these wider cultural movements make it clear that the prescription for theologically healthy congregations is not simple. The radical secularization of our culture has deprived us of the *theos* of our theology. The new spirituality seeks to restore the *theos*, but too often in ways that are palatable to the secularized intellect. The result is that it may endanger the *logos* of theology. Postmodernism will annihilate much of what has been dear to Christian doctrinal formulations even as it opens new possibilities for constructive theology. It invites the *theos* but conceived by means of a new *logos*.

Theological Reflection for a New Century

A book on preaching doctrine for a new century must take seriously the kind of theological thought and discourse that is possible and relevant for those of us living in a century that promises to be postmodern. To suggest that preaching doctrine in the twenty-first century can revert to the homiletical style of Augustine, Luther, Wesley, or even Fosdick is naïve. We propose that theological reflection in this new century will likely have several distinguishing qualities, some of which are already discernible in contemporary theology and homiletics.

The Framing of Experience

First, theological reflection in the new century will address the issue of the framework of experience. Our assumption is that the most postmodern of our congregations will care little, if any, about doctrine as it has been traditionally understood. They will identify such thought with all that which has been demolished by the changes that have transpired in their worlds. The fact that Athanasius or Luther propagated this or that idea may be of some historical interest to them, but alone will not persuade them that the idea is worthy of their consideration. In effect, historical arguments alone may not avail us anything in the theological formation of the congregation (although, as we will see, that will not free us of knowing our tradition).

What we believe will be of interest to our listeners, regardless of their location in the swirl of cultural change, is something that has possibilities as a structure of reference for their experience. This suggestion supposes that there is already, and will increasingly be, a kind of fundamental pragmatism inherent in most of our listeners. If it sounds as if it will work to order their lives, they will attend to it.

We propose that North Americans are desperate for a framework, a perspective, a worldview, that enables them to make sense out of their ordinary, daily experience. In our secularized society at the close of the twentieth century, life suffered dismemberment, the likes of which may not yet be fully understood. Life and experience became atomized, broken into tiny pieces, each unrelated to the others. A holism was lost as the general fabric of North American society came unraveled and as life became so much more complicated than it ever was for our parents and grandparents. The result is that our listeners, and we ourselves, tend to experience life in small units of meaning (see chapter 5). Within themselves those units may have some semblance of cohesiveness, but those segments of experience do not cohere with one another. For instance, people may find their work, or a certain part of it, a unit of experience but have trouble relating what they do at work to family life. Devout Christian laity may find their experience in the church fulfilling but be unable to relate it to the rest of their lives—work, family, or friends.[12]

What is lacking is an overarching structure within which to interpret all of these dismembered pieces of life. Life lacks a whole picture, a total pattern that knits the threads of experience into whole fabric. To change the metaphor, the doors and windows, the walls and the roof, the electrical outlets and the lights of a building are meaningless unless they are joined together by a basic framework. On that framework each of the individual parts finds a place and a use—each makes sense when integrated together through the framework. It is the framework of life that is missing for a lot of our listeners.[13]

Doctrinal framing occurs when the preacher's words conjure an image that might hold the fragments of life together. But such framing requires imagination. Humans are able to conceive their lives holistically only by imagining a holistic perspective. This means that imaginative preaching will be required, for the preacher must image anew how God language can unify the listener's experience. But, further, such preaching will invite the listeners themselves to imagine their lives within a theological image.

Preaching doctrine in a new century then will entail addressing the framework of life through provocative and inviting images. The preacher will understand theology to be essentially about a structural reference into which all experience can be fitted and through which it is interpreted. Framing life's experience is the new mode of theology for the new century. The Christian gospel, we contend, is the offer of just such a perspective. If postmodernism takes a nihilistic turn in the course of the first decades of the twenty-first century, the framing of life will become even more difficult for more people. The challenge of preaching into this new century is to present the Christian gospel in imaginative ways that empower listeners to find therein structures to understand the morsels of their life experience. But how we present that possibility and how we facilitate that empowerment become the next crucial issues.

Concreteness and Specificity

Therefore, second, theological reflection for a new century will be concrete and specific rather than abstract and general. Having spoken of the general, overarching framework for life's experience, we need now to recognize that the gospel framework is powerfully known and experienced only as it is enfleshed in concrete and specific language. The listener has to be helped to see the way in which the sermon's message is lived out. Specifically, how is it that what you are saying, preacher, frames my concrete and particular experiences into a whole? So, for instance, to speak of God's grace in Christ as the framework for experience is not adequate in itself. We will ask to see that vague assertion made concrete. The message of the framing quality of grace is communicated as the preacher shows the listeners real life situations in which grace is experienced and shared. Simply to use an illustration to support a proposition about God's grace is not the point. The message is in the story or the word picture itself, even as illustrations were always conceived in their best use (see chapter 4).

This direction in preaching suggests what homileticians have been saying for some time now about the role of story and imagery in the sermon. They are not decorative icing on the cake, which is itself composed of propositions. They are themselves the substance of the sermon and are what impacts and changes listeners' consciousnesses. Another way of saying this is to claim that the framework is built from the concrete parts, not from precast ideas. But newer trends in homiletics also seem to have anticipated what some are calling postmodernism's distrust of totalities, that is, those grand generalities by which we have tried to live our lives.[14] The postmodernist will know and trust only the specific and the concrete.

Is this not the way we actually build the frames of our lives? Not by backing away from all experience to view the whole as God must view it, but by individual, concrete experiences which we gradually begin to put together until we discern a structure among them. Of course, Jesus did precisely this in his teachings. He spoke consistently of the concrete and specific—most powerfully, perhaps, in his parables. In that way he gradually led his disciples to understand the framework for all of this, namely, the kingdom of God.

But we affirm the importance of a selective use of generalizations. Theological reflection in the sermon requires, at the very least, that we point listeners toward some generalizations. We show them a picture of God's grace in a concrete and specific situation but then we name the reality, grace. Thus we may entice them to consider how this reality frames their lives. However, we do not rush to the generalizations but move through the specific and the concrete to discernment of the whole of the framework (see, for example, suggestions for sermon designs in chapter 6).

Imaginative and Empowering Language

But still further, how do we empower listeners to find the theological framework of their lives? In a century in which language is viewed as the substance itself and not merely a vehicle for substance, theological reflection will take the form of imaginative discourse. And that constitutes the third of the characteristics of theological reflection in a new century.

Through the course of the last half of the twentieth century, we gradually uncovered something about language that may prove to be even more revolutionary than the microchip. The discovery took place on at least two different discernible levels. On the academic and scholarly level, there were those who began to speak of the power of language in new ways. Rooted in existential phenomenology, the importance of hermeneutics emerged until Heidegger could speak of language as "the house of being."[15]

From those roots grew a totally new understanding of language that challenged the assumptions of the modernist view. Language is being, not just the articulation of some ideal truths residing somewhere or the other. Language is more than an arbitrary way of expressing some abstract reality that has a life of its own apart from the language. Language is the reality itself. Words form reality, constitute its essence, and bring it into being. Furthermore, being is revealed in language. The revelation of self is always linguistic in nature. More specifically, this means that we understand *through* language. It is the means by which we encounter the real and find it to be relational. Speaking and hearing have to do with interiority that brings into being what was not.

Nearly contemporaneous with and related to these philosophies of language were movements of a more practical and social kind. Psychologists, feminists, and ethnic groups began speaking of the formative power of language on personality and human consciousness. This discovery paralleled the one made in scholarly circles. Language has power to form being; indeed, language creates being, both individually and socially.[16]

Some commentators on the emerging new self-understanding in North America contend that the importance and role of language defines postmodernism. Whether that is the heart of the spirit of the new century, this much is true: We now understand that language forms human consciousness. So, the language we use in preaching is not incidental to our message. It is our message.[17]

The theological formation of congregations, then, will be accomplished through language, most especially through imaginative and empowering language. Chapter 4 is devoted to story and imagery in preaching, so all we need to establish here is the centrality of language in the new theological reflection. The framing of life's experience is done through the specific words that are used and the way they are articulated. Theological reflection is done through language, and language forms new perspectives on experience.

Translating Tradition

The new role of language in contemporary doctrinal preaching implies a fourth characteristic of theological reflection in the twenty-first century: It will translate tradition into a new cultural idiom for a traditionless people. With all that we have said about the novelty of the new age on the threshold of which we stand, we must acknowledge that theology is not reinvented for the occasion. Doctrine is tradition, having its origin in tradition and having been passed from one generation of Christians to the next. Theology is always traditional, even when it challenges tradition.

But, if postmodern congregations care little about doctrine as it has been traditionally understood, how will theological discourse be possible? One way of understanding the task of preaching doctrine for congregations of new people is to speak of translation of the tradition. Translators must carefully weigh the options they have in one language for rendering what they know in another language. Sometimes words even have to be invented to effect translation. But translation here is understood not simply in terms of finding verbal equivalents, although that may sometimes help. More important is translation as "a 'carrying over' (trans-lating) meaning from one linguistic world or culture to another."[18]

In the case of preaching doctrine in the twenty-first century the tasks are several. First, we discern the fragments of our heritage in the people's language. These are scraps of our ancestors' "house of being"—the bits and pieces of language passed on to us.[19] Recognizing traditional fragments enables us to distance ourselves from the tradition. Distancing facilitates critical reflection. Does this language still work? Does it still perform a role in sustaining Christian life and faith in our society? Or, is it pure baggage, empty of meaning and impotent to frame experience?

Second, we re-language the tradition. Now the traditional is brought near again and reformed for the present. Re-languaging involves speaking the tradition with new words, metaphors, and images that listeners can understand and appropriate. It is language they know but which has never been religious for them. The new expressions invite listeners to participate in this language in new ways. We listen to the language that emerges in this century and determine the equivalencies to traditional doctrinal language. The tradition will need to be remolded in the language of the new people of the new century. This remolding of the tradition in new language recreates the heritage and makes it present in the community. Because language is power, the re-languaging of tradition brings the tradition to new reality in a new age. As Sandra M. Schneiders has put it, "Tradition is the actualizing in the present, in and through language, of the most valued and critically important aspects of the community's experience. . . ."[20]

An example may help. We still hear the expression "the blood of Jesus" used in reference to the atoning benefit of Christ's death. But often the words are hollow and foreign to the believer's real experience. They represent the fragments of a traditional understanding of the atonement. When we recognize them as such, we can then reflect on their adequacy. Are the classic views of atonement meaningful today? Are they laden with cultural associations from another time? If so, we then ask further questions: What are the contemporary possibilities for restating the ransom theory of atonement? Are there more adequate ways of expressing the salvific qualities of the cross?[21] We will re-language the tradition, trying to transplant it in the language and images of our own culture. If language is as important as we have argued it is, then the choice of our words will be careful and precise.

Later we will argue that theological language for the most part, if not entirely, is metaphorical (chapter 4). For now it is enough to suggest only that the translation of the tradition entails the imaginative quest for new metaphors to say what has been said with metaphors in other cultural soil in very different ways. If the atonement was once conceived around the language of the Jewish cultic blood sacrifice, what role does the "blood of Jesus" play in the formation of a theology of the cross in the new century? However that re-languaging is accomplished, it is important to understand that the traditional language may no longer work as it once did, and that the tradition will be best served in new linguistic formulations. Moreover, that reformulation must be done in ways that invite appropriation—ways that provoke imaginative conception from the listeners' own experience.

The translation of tradition is fraught with difficult questions and makes enormous demands of the preacher (see chapter 2). What is the core of that which the tradition attempts to preserve? What is marginal to the tradition? What are the culturally bound expressions in which the tradition is preserved? What is trans-cultural? These are hard questions without simple answers. But they suggest one thing very clearly: Preachers who want to engage the congregation in theological dialogue in a postmodern age must know the tradition that birthed and nourished the central affirmations of the church's faith.

A New Communalism

Now we challenge a long embraced societal tradition for the sake of an even more ancient religious tradition. Theology for a new century will assume and nurture a new communalism in the place of an old, modernistic individualism. The indications that radical North American individualism has run its course are increasing in number, and in the new century we will likely be holding its wake. The very same modernism that occasioned the birth of individualism also raised up one of its children to undermine individualism. The social science movement has persistently revealed the fallacy of isolated individual lives. Now postmodern thinkers are arguing that the very foundation of modernist individualism has fallen, namely, Descartes' claim that individual identity is the only certainty on which to build a truth. The concept of the self is at best questionable, given humanity's social nature.

Christian thought succumbed to the temptations of radical individualism and in some cases still lives happily within that house of cards. Any clergyperson who has tried to cultivate a sense of community within a congregation knows something of the consequences of individualism in the church. We are realizing more and more that the Christian tradition is rooted not so much in privatistic human existence but in corporateness.

On this point the contemporary cultural movements happily intersect with our newer understandings of the communal quality of Christian life.

The preaching of doctrine in the future will be premised on our life together and far less on the individual. That means among other things that we will facilitate theological reflection through searching for a common story that embraces the diversity of our individual lives. A common framework for life will glue us together. Preachers will no longer be content to appeal to individuals to develop their own set of beliefs. They will assume the voice for the whole community in articulating both its plight and its promise. The language of the sermon will empower listeners to unite their lives in the framework of experience embraced by their community of faith.

The responsibility will, however, not be easily fulfilled. We are convinced that radical individualism will fade away, at least as we have known it. But the discovery of the new communalism will not be easy, at least in the next several generations. How will we relate our sense of individual identity with the new communalism? Where will I end and you begin, if we are a corporate being together? Preaching in the new century will point directions, careful to speak communally, but without offering easy answers to the quest for the bridge from what we have been to who we are becoming. Not least of all this issue will figure prominently in what has been traditionally called justification by faith. We will have to rediscover the social dimension of this traditional doctrine in its originator, the apostle Paul, in order to form the theological consciousness of our new listeners.[22]

Preaching as Dialogue

Part of the new communalism is found in the last of the characteristics of theological reflection in the new century. If theological reflection is to take place at all in our preaching during the next several decades, it will take place as dialogue, not monologue. Of course, dialogical or conversational preaching is far from new; it has been a consistent theme in homiletics for several decades. Indeed, Fred Craddock contributed to that trend with what has come to be called inductive preaching.[23] But in the new century preacher-congregation interchange will become an absolute necessity. One homiletician who writes about preaching in a postmodern age takes this as her primary emphasis, preferring the word *conversation* to what we are calling dialogue.[24]

The sermon as a monologue may be experiencing its last days. To be sure, there are currently remarkable stories of church growth in which the congregation is treated as spectators at a grand performance.[25] But the generations brought up on computer games and interactive television will no longer find it meaningful to be talked at for fifteen minutes. Congregations will expect to be engaged as partners in the sermonic experience and will reject the role of spectator should that be implied by the preacher's style.

What forms the dialogical preaching will take in the new century are yet unclear. Our guess is that they will continue to range over a wide spectrum. At the one end of the spectrum will be the preacher who invites the congregation to join him or her in reflecting on an issue or an experience, the preacher who proceeds inductively to keep the congregation engaged in the work left for them to do in their own minds. At the other end of the spectrum dialogical preaching may take more radical forms in which there are actual verbal exchanges between the preacher and members of the congregation. Somewhere in this mix, preaching doctrine in the future will doubtless learn still more from the tradition of American black preaching, in which the sermon has always been understood to be a dialogue between the preacher and the congregation.[26]

One conclusion, however, is probably safe. Preachers will accept their role as a colleague in search with the congregation. Doctrinal preaching will no longer consist of the preacher's telling the congregation what they should believe. Rather, congregations will ask their preachers to share with them their quest for life's meaning and purpose.[27] Preachers will speak the search on their behalf and share with the congregation in the discovery of frameworks of reference for life's experience.

These characteristics of preaching doctrine in a new century are admittedly speculative in many ways. We do not pretend to have an inerrant crystal ball. But we offer these as an effort to capture something of the spirit of the age that is upon us and how it looks and feels from the pulpit.

Conclusion: The Renewal of Doctrine Preaching

This chapter has attempted to set the stage for our investigation of preaching doctrine in the new century. We have suggested that there is an increasing need for theological formation among the laity. We then undertook to understand that need in the context of three wider cultural movements. That led us to postmodernism and the attempt to describe the characteristics of theological reflection in such an age, especially as it relates to preaching.

All of this points us toward the necessity for a renewal of doctrinal preaching, but of a doctrinal preaching that will take new forms. In what follows we hope to suggest ways in which preaching for theological formation can be done with both cultural sensitivity and faithfulness to our calling. Preaching will continue to be the proclamation of the gospel—the good news of what God has done for us in Christ. It will continue to be radically biblical and will be shaped by the most recent understandings of communication. But preaching doctrine for a new century will need to provide our new listeners access to the central doctrines of the faith and show how those doctrines are rooted in contemporary human experience. How that might be done is the subject of the following chapters.

2

Toward a Homiletic Theology
for a New Century

Gerhard Forde has written a provocative volume entitled *Theology Is for Proclamation.*[1] There he argues that theology, properly understood, is for the sake of proclamation. This book helps the preacher in a number of significant ways, not least of all by going to the heart of a doctrine to articulate it in terms of what ought to be preached.

But we want to reverse Forde's title to claim that *proclamation is for theology.* We will reflect on the way in which preaching has as one of its purposes the articulation of theological themes. The essential purpose of preaching, of course, is always the proclamation of the gospel. But how is it that theology plays a role in the announcement of the good news? From this perspective we will explore the ways in which theology and preaching are related to each other, the purpose of theology in preaching, and how it is integrated into the sermon.

We continue the focus of the final section of chapter 1 by asking how theological reflection might be done in the sermon, but now with a sharper concentration on what we will call homiletic theology. We want to begin reflection on a method for homiletic theology appropriate to the emergence of a new century. By this we mean the way in which theological reflection is done for the sake of contemporary preaching. A homiletic theology addresses how the preacher theologizes in sermon preparation and in the sermon itself. More formally, homiletic theology is the articulation of basic Christian doctrine in the context of the sermon.[2] But the exploration into the precise nature of homiletic theological reflection of a new century must be continued. First, we must raise two preliminary questions in preparation for a more specific treatment of homiletic theology.

The Nature and Purpose of Theology in General

The discipline of theology has been variously defined in accord with the time and cultural context. We offer, not an exhaustive definition, but only a suggestion for theology's point of origin: *Christian theology begins with reflection on the good news of what God has done in Christ.* Such a minimalist suggestion, however, implies a number of important features of theology for the preacher.[3]

First, our proposal for theology's point of origin is, in the truest sense of the word, evangelical and christocentric in that it focuses exclusively on the *euangelion* resulting from God's act in Christ. Our assumption is that all Christian theology begins there—that even a doctrine of creation takes the Christ event as its vantage point. While such a view of theology may suffer the weakness of radical christocentricity at the expense of the first and third persons of the Trinity, we maintain that it is with the salvific action of God that Christian theological reflection must begin. We acknowledge the gospel of the Hebrew Scriptures in and of themselves, but recognize too that Christians invariably read even the good news of God's activity in Israel's history in the light of the Christian gospel.

A good news orientation to theology means, however, that the discipline is *systematic*. It seeks through cognitive powers and imaginative insight to explore the logical implications of the gospel and the rational connections among the aspects of the good news. As Paul Scott Wilson summarizes it, all forms of systematic theology are concerned to "test the logical consequences of any doctrinal position."[4] So, for instance, reflection on what God has done in Christ rationally leads us to consider a range of issues: The identity of Jesus, the meaning of the cross and resurrection, the relationship between God's redemption and creation, and the relationship between history and faith. The gospel is the vestibule of the temple of Christian theology with its endless rooms. Theology is, then, holistic in terms of its effort to understand the interrelatedness of the Christ event and the whole of existence.

By *doctrine* we mean only a discrete subject or theme in the whole of a theology. The word sometimes connotes the church's absolutist formulations of the faith. Doctrine equals dogma. Dogma equals undebatable. Without any such connotations we use doctrine as a way of speaking of a focus of reflection on the gospel—one distinct part of the whole of theology. Of course, doctrine is related inescapably to Christian tradition. But a doctrine is always to be understood within a broader system with each theme or focus related to all others.

More important for preaching, our proposal for the genesis of theology intends to imply that *theological reflection is rooted in the experience of the gospel*.[5] That is, those who have been affected by the gospel message are interested in reflecting on it. We who claim to have been gospeled are they who are responsible for reflecting on the good news. Theology is, then, properly the work of the church, as Barth so strongly insisted. Theological reflection is the cognitive and imaginative process of finding the intersections between God's act in Christ and our own existence. How is that act known and embraced? How does that act affect human existence? Where in experience is the locus of the gospel?

Obviously we mean by experience the whole human consciousness of existence, not emotion or cognition alone. We engage in theology as beings conscious of our own existence with memories of the past and anticipations of the future. In this sense, then, theological reflection involves examining the relationship between our conscious existence and the gospel message. For instance, if we reflect on the relationship between God's redemption in Christ and creation, we are led to reflect on our own experience of both the created order and disorder of things, with all the despair that conjures in us, as well as the ultimate redemption of the whole of the created order, arising from a fundamental hope. Theology assumes that reflection on God's act has always been done in relation with human experience, and in this way experience becomes one of the resources for theological reflection, along with Scripture and reason.

Theological reflection is, therefore, holistic in at least two ways: in exploring the whole of the implications of the gospel, and the whole of the relationship between the gospel and human existence. Such a holistic understanding of the theological task will undergird any sound homiletic theological method.

But what, then, is the purpose of theology in the sermon? We need to delineate a number of different purposes theology may play in preaching. Let us begin with the observation that the very act of preaching assumes a theology. One who preaches presupposes a view of the proclamation of the gospel. Why preach at all? What is the purpose of preaching? The act of proclamation arises from a reflection on the gospel. It supposes that the articulation of the gospel message is in some sense a fundamental means by which the gospel does its work in the lives of the listeners. There are always theologically grounded purposes for preaching, whatever they may be and however unreflective the preacher may be about them. The very act of preaching is already an implicit theological statement.[6]

The theology of preaching is an oft-neglected topic in recent decades, since the gradual demise of the popularity of the theology of the Word. That fact has left a dangerous vacuum in the church. On the one hand, the space best occupied by a theology of preaching is a void into which many a preacher's life and calling have collapsed. Without a substantive view of preaching, homiletical burnout is all the more likely. The preacher is haunted by debilitating questions: How can my preaching compete with the glamour of the media? Why preach when it seems to make so little difference to my congregation? Why should I spend time on sermon preparation with all the other pressing obligations thrust on me by ordained parish ministry?

The other vacuum left by the absence of clear theologies of preaching is found among our listeners. They have little sense of why they should listen to preaching—especially if we equally have little idea. There is, among a good many of the laity at least, a widespread misunderstanding as to why pastors preach. Is it for entertainment while we worship? Is it strictly to teach the Bible? Is it to give guidance for Christian living? Is it to win souls for Christ? Given this absence of understanding, might we not be more intentional about helping the laity consider the theological purpose of preaching? In spite of the absence of clear, articulate theologies of preaching, each sermon we preach asserts a theological claim: preaching is worthwhile in God's redemptive plan.

But, further, every sermon—indeed, every movement within a sermon—presupposes theology.[7] Preaching is an interdisciplinary task, of which theological reflection is a primary ingredient. Indeed, the composition of the sermon is a profoundly theological task. Sermons are comprised at least of these elements: the biblical text, the situation of the congregation, understandings of communication, and, of course, specific content. Each of these involves sophisticated theological reflection.

The struggle with *the text* involves reading it through and sometimes over against theological presuppositions. Our hermeneutic is invariably colored by theological presuppositions. It is never pure of our own beliefs. So, the first theological task may be that of becoming aware of our presuppositions as interpreters. But further, interpreting the text always involves discernment and understanding of the theological motifs of the text (see chapter 3). For example, in John 5:28 Jesus declares, "The hour is coming when all who are in the tombs will hear the Son of Man's voice and come forth, those who have done good, to the resurrection of life, and those who have done evil, to the resurrection of judgment." We may come to this text presupposing justification by grace, not works, and want to dilute the text of its power. Interpreting the text honestly, we must ask a theological question: How are works related to God's final destiny for humans? The text calls for thorough examination in its context and reflection on several important doctrines.

But theological assumptions are also involved in considering *the situation of the congregation*. What are the theological implications of the situation of this congregation? How does one assess their condition in the light of reflection on the gospel? For instance, how does one assess theologically the hopelessness of a dying inner-city congregation? Does a theology of the cross cast their situation in a different light? Has a theology of glory operated in their consciousness to nurture a sense of failure? When all the sociological analysis of the congregation and their community is completed, we are still left asking what that means in the light of the gospel.

Even *theories of communication* have their theological implications. How we seek to communicate our message entails our doctrine of human nature. How do I understand the nature of my listeners? But other questions are also theological: Does my theology of preaching sanction the manipulation of listeners' emotions (perhaps with a tear-rendering story) for the sake of the gospel? Does my understanding of the gospel endorse the use of story as a medium for proclamation? Does my theology lead me to preach primarily for cognitive understanding, emotional experience, or empowerment of the will?

Of course, theology is involved in the determination of the *content of the sermon* as a whole and in its individual fragments. Given my understanding of prayer and the nature of God's involvement in the world, what is the promise of prayer I can with integrity proclaim to the congregation? Can I say, without qualification, that petitions will be granted somehow in God's good time? Can I encourage praying for healing? For good and plentiful harvest? For the success (or failure) of a political party? Or, what is the relationship between the gospel itself and the moral imperative of the gospel? Does the announcement of the gospel always necessitate the exhortation for the listeners to do something? Is there a way I can articulate a costly grace without nurturing a works righteousness? At every turn in the sermon, in every fragment of the sermon, theological considerations loom large.

Preaching, then, has to do with theological reflection, whether or not one is intentionally preaching doctrine. Indeed, every sermon and each fragment of every sermon is theological in nature, often times consciously so, but perhaps sometimes unconsciously. Preaching is a profoundly theological task.

The Nature and Form of Homiletic Theology

With these preliminary questions addressed, the next question has to do with the more specific nature of the theology in which we engage when preaching. What form of theologizing is called for in the sermon? Our discussion will assume the remarks made in the previous chapter with regard to the nature of theological reflection in a postmodern age but will attempt to contextualize those assertions in a broader understanding of the method of homiletic theology. To do so, we delineate five characteristics of homiletic theology.

First, in its method a homiletic theology overcomes a faulty separation of didache and kerygma. This separation originated in the form-critical studies of the New Testament. It was intended to distinguish certain literary types from others. C. H. Dodd argued that this form distinction was evident in Acts, among other places, and the distinction proved very helpful in the analysis of New Testament literature.[8] But then that form-critical distinction crept into our understanding of the ministry of the church, as well, and was expanded into a general principle. By that principle we are to distinguish between the efforts to proclaim the gospel and teach about the life of faith. The distinction between preaching and teaching is useful in many ways. But the absolutizing of the distinction demands more of it than was ever intended.

To distinguish teaching sharply from preaching is simplistic and dangerous for a number of reasons. It is only partially accurate with regard to the representations of early Christian preaching found in the New Testament. Teaching is frequently integral to the samples of early preaching we have in the New Testament. Peter's Pentecost sermon in Acts 2, for instance, uses a basic Jewish teaching device—interpretation of Scripture, namely, Joel and Psalms. The interpretation of those passages was a kind of teaching integral to the sermon. Hence, it appears that teaching was part of the preaching of the earliest Christians.

The distinction between kerygma and didache is also simplistic from the perspective of how people hear the gospel. To hear the gospel entails the mind as well as the emotions and the will. The Word addresses the whole person. Therefore, it is not devoid of cognitive content. To distinguish the cognitive entirely from the emotional and volitional violates the holism of a person and falls into the modernist trap of distinction. One contribution to postmodern thought is the critique of the modernist ideology of difference. Against that ideology critics have proposed a criterion of unity.[9] A holism of teaching and preaching moves toward a postmodern mode of proclamation.

Preaching, therefore, is always teaching. We always teach something in our preaching. We do this implicitly whether we intend to or not. Every time we use synonyms to help people understand us, we teach. With each metaphor to help them understand or become engaged, we teach. Each time we tell a story to stimulate their imaginations, we teach. For instance, even the innocent statement that we and the congregation have been blessed with material abundance implicitly teaches a view of the transcendent and our experience. Such an innocent acknowledgment of our dependence on God's goodness may teach the image of God as one who blesses some with money and curses others with poverty.

So, we need to ask of every sermon, what is being taught here? Whether the sermon intends to be didactic, or whether didactic is the last word we would use to characterize the sermon, it will teach. What will the sermon teach by suggestion, inference, or insinuation?

This is especially the case regarding stories used in sermons (see chapter 4). Story tends to frame the experience of people, to provide roots, orientation, direction to life, even when we may have intended the story only as a vehicle of a propositional statement. Our stories will be taken into lives as tales of consciousness by which we may live. This is all the more true if people are searching for new stories to frame their existence, as our earlier analysis of cultural trends suggests. If the story of individualism is dying, will our stories nurture a new corporate mentality? Like the whole of our preaching, stories will teach, whether we want them to or not.

Our task, then, is to ask what our sermons teach. Indeed, the mandate of faithfulness requires us to ask this question, all the more so, if our listeners are in search of new meaning for their lives in a new age.

In doing homiletic theology—theological reflection in and for preaching—we overcome the separation of kerygma and didache and take seriously the teaching-learning of the sermon experience. Of course, this is not to say that there are no differences between the two. But it is to surmount the dangers of compartmentalization.

If we overcome this faulty distinction and recognize the teaching potential of preaching, we must also ask how teaching is done through our preaching. We will address this question only briefly here and return to it in later chapters. For now, consider the following means of teaching through preaching, formulated by and adapted from the work of Ronald J. Allen:[10]

a. Through the relationship between the preacher and the congregation in which the preacher is trusted as teacher and guide and in turn, the preacher trusts the congregation to search for themselves.

b. Through the preacher's nurturing the listeners' sense of participation in the sermon.

c. Through the use of cognitive dissonance and questions. This assumes that when the preacher creates cognitive dissonance in the listeners and raises questions for them, they follow him or her in the search for resolution (see chapters 5 and 6).

d. Through creating and highlighting coherence in the content of the subject of the sermon.

e. Through modeling a method for learning and thinking.

f. Through dealing creatively with resistance to learning. When the congregation resists learning, the preacher seeks creative ways of enticing them into their roles as disciples (that is, learners).

In these ways, among others, the preacher may be able to unite proclamation and learning, and become effective in both.

Second, through language, homiletic theology bridges and reformulates experience and abstraction. We learn to think about theology in abstractions, and so we speak of concepts, ideas, and foci. Theology becomes intellectual exercises designed to find the heart of our faith and the interrelatedness of its components. All of this is proper and good. But homiletic theology demands that we discern and articulate experiential theology. It moves not strictly in the realm of the abstract, but names the abstract at points where what was thought to be abstract is lived, experienced, and known with immediacy. Homiletic theology locates and identifies the substance of living doctrine. For instance, what does it mean experientially to say that the risen Christ lives among us?

The communal experience of the earliest Christians is the beginning point of all Christian theology. Theological reflection began for them in a shared new consciousness. They sensed that a new age had begun, as

Buttrick so well argues.[11] They shared their lives together in community, and reflected on what that shared experience meant. They tried to name their experience, to bring it into new reality through language, often the language of metaphor. For example, the high view of Christ developed gradually in New Testament history, and along the way we find numerous expressions of Christ's identity. (Compare, for instance, the role of the birth narratives in Matthew and Luke with their absence in Mark and John.) The church's christology does not arise from nothingness, as if revealed from the heavens. The early Christians moved through a long process of languaging their communal reflections on who this Jesus was and is. Their language gave new reality to both their experience and their reflections. You could say the later church did the same thing. They tried to recreate through words their shared experience of Christ and eventually arrived at the Chalcedonian formulation.

So, the sermon's language does several things. First, it names human experience, and in so doing recreates that experience into new reality. But, second, it names abstraction in relation to experience. By doing that, an old abstraction dies, and a new experienced abstraction is born. In "Preaching as Lively Teaching" Hughes writes, ". . . it is essential to get behind doctrines to their related human experience."[12] By speaking freshly of experience and abstraction, preaching makes experience new and names doctrine that resides in the listeners' immediate present. Hence, old theological abstractions relate to people's real experiences, whether in the workplace, in the home, or in the shopping mall.

This does not denigrate abstraction and conceptualization. Our listeners (we ourselves) need concepts to hold our experience together, as we have argued in chapter 1. Experience is fragmented. Meaning for life comes in identifying images and concepts that unite the fragments of experience. Conceptuality is then a framework for a life, that is, a total view of all of life and reality that gives meaning to their individual parts. And homiletic theology seeks just such conceptuality—conceptuality, if you will, for life. It seeks to help listeners find possible ways of framing the whole of their experience.[13]

So, homiletic theology moves dialectically between experience and conceptuality. Sometimes we begin with naming the concept, then move to languaging experience; sometimes we begin with experience, then rename it by speaking of it as a broader concept. New experience is set within new concepts. Concepts are transformed with experience, and experience with concepts.

Such a dialectic might look this way in a sermon design on 2 Corinthians 4:7. Paul speaks of Christian life as having a treasure in an earthen vessel. The sermon begins with speaking of the frailty of life. It is easily broken like the cheap bowls made of clay used in the temple. What would it mean to hold a treasure within such a frail vessel? What if the treasure were the sense that your Creator had deemed human life priceless and precious? To this point attention has been on naming the experience of life's frailty and being loved by God. Now the preacher recreates those with different words: We are both saints and sinners at the same time. Saints because God has sanctified us with love; sinners because we continue to be frail, cracked pots. And through language, the preacher has bridged and reformulated experience (life broken, yet treasured) and abstraction (saints and sinners at the same time). This feature of homiletic leads us to another that involves language.

Third, homiletic theology seeks to re-language and re-image tradition. We argued in chapter 1 that tradition will become increasingly irrelevant in a postmodern age. Consequently, theological reflection will need to seek ways of translating tradition into the language of the people in order to reformulate the heart of tradition in fresh ways. Here we hope to elaborate on what is required of a homiletic theology that accomplishes this purpose.

The first requirement is that preachers themselves know the tradition. We mentioned some of the questions this task raises for the preacher. Translators must know the original language, as well as the new language into which they hope to render the original. This means that homiletic theologians are required to know the Christian tradition from the inside. In this case, the inside means knowing what the traditional doctrine expressed was and the cultural metaphors and language that were used in formative articulations of the doctrine. The homiletic theologian will need to be a far better historical theologian than many of us were trained to be.

Let us use another example from the theology of the cross. The satisfaction theory of atonement was constructed with the metaphor of relations between the serf and the lord of the land in medieval culture. The lord is offended by the serf's wrongdoing, and his honor must be satisfied by some sort of compensation. So, the atonement was understood in terms of the degree to which God had been offended by human sin and the necessity of satisfying the divine honor. Christ's death was, in this view, the compensation paid to God for human sin.

Obviously, the metaphor no longer works. Ours is not a medieval culture dominated by lords and their honor. The cultural confinements of the theory are clear; but the question is, what did the core of the theory affirm? Perhaps the strength of the satisfaction theory is its emphasis on the costliness of redemption. God's justice could not simply be ignored; humanity's offense against its Creator could not be taken lightly. Our society continues to believe that severe injustice cannot go unnoticed; justice must be served, as we are inclined to say. Yet in God's act in Christ, God bore the cost of redemption in God's own self. God took the cost into the divine self, specifically, in the death of the divine Son. The doctrinal center of the satisfaction theory of atonement is the relationship between love and justice in God's actions, and the homiletic theologian will discern that center and reflect on it in the congregation's own language and images. The result might be a story or an image of one who has been offended by injustice but who corrects that injustice through self-sacrificial love.

Translating traditional doctrine for the congregations of the new century will require homiletic theologians who know the tradition. But that delicate task will also require that the homiletic theologian know the congregation. If translators must know the language into which they will render the original language, preachers will need to know the language and culture of their hearers. This will entail exegesis of a congregation comparable to the exegesis we do of a text for preaching. Listening to the congregation is as important as listening to the text. Such listening will require that homiletic theologians know their congregation's faith and the language it frequently uses of its faith. What is their story and to what degree does it still work for them?

A seminary student once did a study of a congregation that believed the assumption that its membership had declined due to former members' cowardice about facing the realities of their changing neighborhood. He had heard member after member tell this story, conveniently blaming and condemning the former members. Using that story the remaining congregation explained their weakness in ministry, their financial struggle to make ends meet, and their stubborn refusal to close their church. The student, however, did a careful study of the former members. He learned that the vast majority of these people did not move to a suburb and transfer their memberships to a congregation there. The membership decline was due to transfers that are generally regarded as normal; it just happened that a large number of these transfers took place in a short period of time. The student realized that the congregation's story was based on a misconstrual of the evidence and served as a way to protect their status quo. Theologically the story worked to transfer responsibility for the church's mission to convenient scapegoats and facilitate a denial of the realities of the present congregation's situation.

Carefully listening to a congregation's own peculiar story provides entry into their self-understanding with all of its certainties and doubts, its hopes and disappointments, and its strengths and weaknesses. Whatever a congregation's level of theological sophistication, their articulations of their faith are part of who they are as a community of faith. To some degree or another, the way laity speak of their faith expresses their experience as Christians. Every doctrine we attempt to explore through preaching needs to be woven into the congregation's story and the language by which it understands itself.

Suppose, for example, that the text leads us to reflect in our sermon on the experience of alienation. A rural congregation knows alienation from one another in a distinctively different way than do urban or suburban congregations. Alienation may not take the form of not knowing your neighbors, as is so often the case in suburban settings; but it may express itself in secretly held disdain for certain others whom you greet with a smile each time you meet them. Pastors/homiletic theologians listen to the hints of such brokenness in the words of parishioners and translate the doctrine of human alienation in terms of what they have heard.

But homiletic theologians also know themselves with brutal honesty. William Muehl has expressed this point well. "The person preparing to go into the pulpit is required to ask probing questions of himself or herself about the real meaning of those familiar formulations in a world that differs so markedly from the one in which so much doctrine took shape."[14] This means that we must ask ourselves some fundamental questions: What is my own theological stance? How important do I think theological understanding really is? How real is this doctrine to me? Does it articulate experience or is it lifeless abstraction? Coming to some honest self-understanding in response to questions like these is an essential prerequisite for preaching doctrine. We ourselves may not have integrated a particular doctrine with our own experience.

One of us was once confessing his own reservations about the doctrine of divine providence to a dear friend and colleague in ordained ministry. The friend replied, "Bob, I have experienced more providence in my life than I believe in." In some ways that characterizes the kind of self-knowledge required for preaching doctrine in the new mode demanded of us in the twenty-first century.

Self-knowledge relates to another requirement for homiletic theology, namely, the avoidance of hollow language. Hollow language denotes nothing in specific. It is inauthentic speech; it uses words in infinitely interchangeable ways, and does little more than fill the silences of our lives. Hollow language is often language that was once meaningful, but which now has become empty for our listeners and probably for us. But the words linger on in our speech. What has been emptied of meaning depends a great deal, for us, on our own tradition and Christian journey and, for the congregation, on its own story and tradition. For instance, the word *spiritual* is often used with a carelessness that suggests hollowness. If some of these words and expressions are used, the preacher's task is to fill them with new meaning, which means that we may have to find new meanings for ourselves.

Finally, homiletic theology obviously requires imagination. We will speak of the role images play in preaching doctrine in chapter 4. For now it is enough to say that translating tradition entails inventing new languages and images for old treasures. If in our concept of the cosmos we know there really is no up or down, how shall we speak of Christ's ascension? If we know that the Lukan story of Christ's ascension is linked with his exaltation, how do we re-image that theme? With the popularity of science fiction, is it possible to speak of different cosmic realms? Can we better language Christ's departure in terms of transference to another realm than of rising up into the heavens? Homiletic theologians play with such possibilities in search of new images for a precious tradition. Imagination becomes an invaluable tool in such an endeavor.[15]

Fourth, homiletic theology is essentially local theology. In recent decades, Christians living outside the Western, Eurocentric world have developed methods for doing theology appropriate to their cultural settings.[16] A local theology is one that begins reflection with the realities of life for the laity; its first step is to name that which is indigenous to the laity's world, for example, a life of poverty and oppression. Local theology takes seriously and actually roots theological reflection in the people's situation. Their condition is as valuable for theology as are the traditional creeds of the church, and in a sense even more valuable since the people's situation constitutes the beginning point of discourse. So, local theology is reflection from below, meaning that it uses the real life situation of people as its foundation. Rather than beginning from above—with God and the divine actions—it begins with human realities.

In sum, local theology is reflection on the gospel that is integral to the lives of a congregation's laity. Homiletic theology is in this sense always local theology. It is theology for a specific people of God, in one place at one time, and theologizing for this particular congregation in their language and in the light of their experience. The attention paid to listening to the congregation is not simply for the purpose of making the gospel relevant; it provides a basic ingredient for the theological mix.

Homiletic theology is postmodern in this regard. The preacher never assumes that she or he has spoken universal truth for all humans of every time and place, but only truth for now for this particular community of Christians. Homiletic theology avoids claims of universalism, with some notable exceptions essential to the gospel itself. These notable exceptions are the points at which Christian theology may never be fully postmodern, at least in terms of some of the most current and radical formulations of postmodernism.

Perhaps you have had an experience we share, namely, a sense that your sermons are so very restricted. Seldom can we preach an old sermon again, because it was written for a particular situation. Moreover, sometimes we feel intimidated by the thought that a professional theologian might accidentally hear that sermon. But good sermons have that quality about them, and that is what homiletic theology is.[17]

But, if our homiletic theologizing is local and aimed at producing a working theology, this means that we preachers are always doing a kind of fresh, new, and unprecedented theology. It is a theology for real life in the workplace or in the home and is not confined to an academic audience. In that way, it is basic theology in the sense that it arises from and speaks to the real life conditions of a specific congregation. Without demeaning formal and academic theology, we maintain that much of the most creative theological reflection occurs when the pastor/preacher represents the congregation in reformulating basic Christian tenets for living. On behalf of the laity, homiletic theology seeks to language the faith in new and relevant ways, and for that reason is by its nature both sensitive to the full range of human experience and creative in its reflection on the relationship of the gospel to that gamut of experience.

Hence, homiletic, local theology has a dual relationship with systematic or constructive theology. On the one hand, preaching depends on scholarly, professional theology. We draw from it, use it, and even require it. On the other hand, preaching is doing theology afresh, articulating the faith in terms of the experience of this local culture in this particular time and place. Only the resident theologian—the preacher/pastor—can do that. This lifts preaching and homiletic theology to a new level. Stories, images, metaphors, turns of phrases are sought as ways of giving voice to the uniqueness of Christian life in a particular place. We birth symbols that recreate concepts—symbols by which a particular community of Christians can live and move and have their being. Preaching is one of the primary means by which we enable congregations to discern their place in the world and the meaning of their existence. The preacher/pastor/local theologian is the congregation's primary theologian, and we in turn enable the baptized to live and see in theological ways. This leads us to a final feature of homiletic theology.

Fifth, homiletic theology seeks the theological formation of the people of God.[18] Homiletic theology is public theologizing done for a local situation. But as such it models how the laity might reflect on the gospel for themselves. That is, the way we do theology in the pulpit ought to be the way laity can think about their lives in relationship with their faith.

An instance of what we have in mind might occur when we reflect on the theological significance of an experience of the betrayal of friendship. Suppose we tell a personal story about our own experience of having been betrayed by a friend, and then we reflect on what that experience means for us in terms of our faith. The way we do that reflection ought to model for our listeners how they, too, might consider their similar experiences. Betrayal suggests the way in which sin and brokenness pervade our lives and our relationships; perhaps it suggests the difficulties many of us have in learning to trust another; maybe it hints at our need for something or someone we can trust without reserve.

In chapter 4 we will propose how preachers might reflect theologically on story, and in chapter 5 we will explore moments of theological reflection in the sermon, so we refer you for now to those discussions. In general, however, the purpose of theological reflection in the pulpit is, among other things, to empower listeners to do their own theological reflection. Its goal is to demonstrate how the laity might reflect on their lives in terms of their Christian discipleship. The purpose is to equip the saints to understand themselves and their world in the light of the gospel. In the simplest of terms, homiletic theology attempts to form lay theologians.[19]

That goal is part of a larger theme in homiletic theology, namely, to foster the consciousness of the congregation as a people of God. The purpose of theology in the pulpit is to nurture a transformed consciousness that shapes the perception and understanding of experience in terms of God's redemptive act in Christ. The task actually entails the implantation of a hermeneutic of life—a method of reading experience. Put another way, homiletic theology seeks to empower the congregation to reformulate the relationship between faith and life, between Sunday morning and the rest of the week, between church and the workplace, and between our vocation as Christians and our vocations as employees, parents, and children. Homiletic theology is about the task of forming a hodgepodge of individuals into the body of Christ.[20]

Conclusion

In several ways then, proclamation *is* for theology. Theology is at the heart of sound and faithful preaching. It undergirds the act of preaching itself and is either implicitly or explicitly the content of every sermon. But the sort of theologizing preachers do is peculiar, and to that peculiar form of theology we give the name homiletic theology. Theology in the sermon is doing fresh and local theology for a new people of God. Preaching doctrine is really not a matter of choice. The only choice involved is whether we do it well and intentionally or poorly and unintentionally.

3

Getting to Know the Text

If chapters in books had theme songs, this chapter's would be, "Getting to Know You," since we want to suggest ways in which preachers can get to know the theology of a text. Any homiletic theology takes Scripture as it basic authority, however that authority might be construed. Therefore, the preacher never sets out to preach doctrine without some use of the Christian canon as a basic source. The new century will doubtless challenge afresh the authority of Scripture. But we remain committed to biblical preaching, especially when the goal is preaching for the laity's theological formation.

The theological content of the best of sermons begins with and is consistent with the biblical text itself. With the possible exception of a doctrinal series of sermons, we preach the theology of the biblical passage, and biblical passages are always theological. Sound biblical preaching is always theological, and sound theological preaching is always biblical. Therefore, homiletic theology is in every case biblical theology. If some preaching has failed effectively in the recent past to nurture the theological formation of the congregation, it may be that the preaching has failed to be soundly biblical.

Consequently, any strictly theological interpretation of the text takes for granted an adequate exegetical method. The task of this chapter is to investigate how we might faithfully interpret a biblical passage for its theological themes. But all that we will say about the interpretation of the text assumes that the whole exegetical process is also part of the study for homiletic theology, for careful exegesis is necessary for a full dialogue with the text.[1] Our purpose is to suggest certain specific stages in the investigation of the text that will especially elucidate the theological content of a passage. But first we must address a preliminary issue.

Theological Presupposition in Exegesis

A classic problem in biblical interpretation since the advent of critical investigation—and one that homiletic theology cannot dodge—is how to exegete a text without imposing our own theological convictions on it. Is it possible to allow the text to speak in its own voice without the distortions of our prejudices? How do we keep our peculiar Christian tradition and its theological perspective from influencing the way we read and understand a passage?

The Demise of Objectivity

Historical critical study of Scripture arose, in part at least, as an effort to wrest the Bible away from the church's dogmatic interpretation. The church had too easily read Scripture in terms of its professed creeds. Critical scholarship after the Enlightenment disrupted that happy marriage between church and Scripture. It attempted to study Scripture without the imposition of dogma.

Finally, of course, modern critical scholarship had to concede that its claims of objectivity in interpretation were nothing but a pretense and that exegesis without presuppositions was a sham.[2] The objective and scientific nature of biblical interpretation that survived for decades finally fell victim to our increasing acknowledgment that no human endeavor is purely objective. Contemporary biblical scholarship has turned sharply away from the claim of its Enlightenment ancestors. The result is that more and more scholarly interpretative articles claim to be no more than a reading of the text—suggesting that the number of possible readings is infinite.[3]

So, the answer to our question, can we interpret Scripture without being influenced by our own theological presuppositions, is a resounding *no*. We never read a text without prejudgments and biases. And in one sense this is as it should be, since we believe that Scripture speaks afresh in each reading, depending on the condition of the readers. There is no interpretation that is purely objective.

In our pursuit of the theological sense of a passage, what then are we to do with our presuppositions? Are we doomed to return to a pre-critical reading of the text, with the assurance that the passage will support our own theological convictions? The questions are especially important when interpretation is focused on theology, for all of us have been trained to find our own tradition's theology in the Bible.

Awareness of Presuppositions

The only recourse we have comes from two resources. The first is to approach the interpretative task with a heightened awareness of our own presuppositions. The more we know ourselves, our convictions, and our predispositions, the better we can control their influence on our reading of the text. Getting to know a text depends in part on knowing ourselves. Many of us have had the experience of realizing that Sunday after Sunday we have managed to find something in the lectionary readings that gave expressions to one of our pet predilections—one of our basic convictions. At that point our suspicions were rightly aroused, and we each spent some time reflecting on our presuppositions.

Coming to the text with awareness of how our theological perspective might influence what we see in the text allows us a limited freedom to transcend those presuppositions. To some measured degree we can suspend our preconceptions and experience the text itself. For example, we might know that our particular Christian tradition has emphasized the importance of individual decision in the process of believing. When we face a text that seems to suggest that faith is predetermined (for example, John 6:44), we can more honestly treat the text if we are aware of our inclination to explain away any hint of predeterminism. Of course that exercise assumes that we wish to read beyond our presuppositions.

Communities of Interpreters

One resource for getting to know the text without imposing our presuppositions on it is an acute sensitivity to our own theological preferences. A second resource is found in a community of interpreters and its capabilities to correct us when we have made the text fit our own presuppositions. The function of biblical commentaries and preaching aids is really to put us in conversation with a larger community of interpreters. Hence, use of such secondary literature serves as a check and balance in our interpretation. (Commentaries seldom provide preachers with much help in formulating sermons, but they will help us avoid distortions of the text.)

But this community of interpreters is still larger. In addition to the literature on the text, that community includes lectionary study groups, conversations with colleagues and congregants, and finally even the whole community of faith.[4] Conversation with others who are committed to interpreting Scripture for Christian life and faith is our best hope for remaining faithful to the actual content of a passage. We listen to what others have to say about the text, and check that against our reading of it.

Biblical interpretation is much like getting to know a stranger. To learn about this other person we try to listen to the other without imposing our prejudices on her or him. We try to ask questions that will elicit informative responses from the other person. Then we may learn how other people perceive this one who is a stranger to us. Do others see them as we do, or is their perception considerably different from our own? Getting to know a text is very similar. We listen, ask the right questions, and then we check with others about the accuracy of our impressions.

Let there be no illusions. These two resources—our awareness of our presuppositions and conversations with wider interpretative communities—will not eliminate the influence of our own presuppositions in the interpretation of a text. But they will provide some protection against the intrusion of eisegesis. This process of seeking awareness of our presuppositions and conversations with others about the text facilitates genuine dialogue with the text, a discourse between us (and our own theological views) and this stranger we call the biblical text. In some cases that conversation will lead to disagreement and even controversy with the text. And such genuine conversation with a passage is the best we can hope for.

Interpretation for Preaching Theological Themes

With full recognition of the ever-present ghost of our own theological preferences, we turn to the process of interpreting biblical texts for their theological themes. Procedures for exegesis are a lot like slicing and serving a plate of fresh fruit to dinner guests. There are many different ways to cut the fruit; there are also many ways to arrange the slices on a plate. But however you slice it and arrange it, the fruit remains the same. The procedure we suggest here shares that feature. There are many ways to divide and arrange the issues in the task.

We hope to propose only some of the essentials involved in elucidating the theological content of a passage. Our suggestion will emphasize four phases in the full exegetical process: (1) Discerning the document's theological motifs through understanding the text in its literary and theological context. (2) Discerning the text's own theological emphases. (3) Imagining with the text. (4) Moving toward the sermon. We will sketch the four-stage process with some examples scattered in along the way, then apply the whole process to a passage to show how it might work.

Discern the Document's Theological Motifs

Conceive of this first step as moving from the outside through three concentric circles. The outer circle represents the whole biblical book in which the passage is found; the middle circle represents the literary unit of which the passage is a part; and the central circle—the target of our inquiry—represents the passage itself. So, each step moves us closer to the passage under investigation.

The outermost circle is a general picture of the theological motifs in the whole book in which our text is found. This first step simply stresses the theological content of the wider context of the passage and has three discrete tasks.

First, we clarify the theological motifs of the document in which the text is found. What are the recurring themes one finds in the whole document? What theological issues does it raise? Here we will try to list all of the themes that have theological importance in the entire book. This may involve working with volumes on the theological or redactional themes of a book, or perhaps volumes on the theologies of the Old and New Testaments.[5] Once we have developed good working lists of such theological themes for the major books of the canon, we file them away carefully so we do not have to reinvent the wheel each week.

Suppose, for instance, that we are working on a passage in the Acts of the Apostles. We will learn that a list of recurring theological themes in Acts looks something like this.

1. The mission of the church.
2. The role and power of witness to the gospel.
3. The empowerment of the Holy Spirit.
4. The role of prayer in the church's life and mission.
5. The religious establishment's resistance to the gospel.
6. The continuity of God's activity in the past in Israel's history and the divine act in Christ.
7. The divine plan for the spread of the gospel.

These themes provide us with a general overview of what Acts stresses and allow us to view our specific passage in their context.

Second, we move into the middle band of the three concentric circles where we clarify the leading theological motifs of the literary unit in which the text is set. What are the theological interests exhibited in the material of the section (a subunit of the whole document) in which the passage is found? To accomplish this task we have to begin by establishing what the larger literary unit surrounding our text is. Where does it begin and where does it end? We check how the commentators have established the boundaries of the unit. Often, however, we will find that commentators do not agree on the perimeters of subunits within a document. So, we will have to decide for ourselves where we think the larger unit begins and where it ends.

Having established the perimeters of the larger literary unit in which our text is set, we attempt to determine what theological themes are featured in it, much as we determined the theological themes of the whole document. What does this portion of the whole book seem to accomplish? What theological ideas are featured in it?

For example, chapter 15 of 1 Corinthians comprises a literary unit unto itself. Paul has addressed a series of issues in the Corinthian church in the earlier chapters. Chapter 15 seems to introduce still another matter about which the Corinthians are confused, and Paul wants to set them straight. "How can some of you say that there is no resurrection of the dead?" (v. 12). Belief in the resurrection of the dead appears to be an issue in the Corinthian church much as speaking in tongues was (1 Corinthians 14:1-40). Chapter 15, however, comprises the conclusion of the substance of the letter. (Chapter 16 is a list of greetings.) Hence, its relation to the rest of the epistle suggests that the issues in chapter 15 reframe everything else Paul has said. Concluding with resurrection places it in a climactic position that allows us to see the discussion in a different light.

The unit (chapter 15) itself stresses these themes:

1. Christ's resurrection.
2. The witnesses of Christ's resurrection appearances (especially Paul's).
3. The resurrection of the believers.
4. The Adam-Christ comparison.
5. The eschatological setting for the resurrection of the believer.

This context allows us to read any portion of the chapter—for example, verses 1-11 on the Fifth Sunday After the Epiphany, series C—within the thematic context of the whole literary unit of which the first eleven verses are a part.

Third, we move to the innermost circle. We set our particular passage down in the context of (1) the theological motifs of the whole document and (2) those in the larger literary unit of which the passage is a part. The task is now to ask a number of questions in the light of the broader literary context in hope of getting to know our text better.

As a beginning we ask, how does our passage appear to contribute to the themes in the larger unit of which it is a part? Does it continue the theological emphasis of the larger unit? Or, does it contribute something new? Within the larger context, is it unique unto itself? Then we broaden our perspective by asking, how does our passage contribute to the theological emphases of the whole document? Or, does it? Is it unique?

The goal of this inquiry is to discover what we learn about the theological nature of a passage in its literary context. The assumption is that seeing a passage in this larger context will allow its peculiar themes to stand out, as well as its themes that support others elsewhere in the book. The passage may replicate or relate to themes in the larger context, or it may introduce ideas that are unprecedented in the rest of the document. In the first case, we can interpret the passage's theological theme in terms of what is said elsewhere about that theme. In the latter case, we can ask why this theme is introduced here and what role it plays if it stands by itself within its literary context.

To return to Acts for an example, let's suppose we are wrestling with 2:1-21 for Pentecost Sunday. We immediately identify in this passage a number of the overarching themes of Acts: In the bestowal of the Spirit (vv. 2-4) we see the empowerment of the Holy Spirit. Peter's words (vv. 14-21) exemplify the role and power of witness to the gospel. His use of the Joel passage (vv. 17-21) suggests the continuity between God's activity in Israel's history and the divine act in Christ. The mission of the church as it is described in Acts is suggested already in the pluralistic nature of the crowd (vv. 5-11).

The passage stands near the beginning of a unit that stretches from 1:15 through 8:3 and narrates the church's witness in Jerusalem and Judea (see 1:8).[6] The unit emphasizes the church's continuation of a number of the aspects of Jesus' own ministry: The proclamation of the reign of God (2:14-36), healing (3:1-10) and other wonders (5:12), prayer (4:23-31), conflict with the religious establishment (4:1-22), persecution (5:17-42), and even death (for example, 7:1-60). But it also sketches the life and mission of the church itself. The unit describes the church's witness again and again (5:27-32) but also its life together

(1:12-14; 2:43-47; 4:32—5:11; and 6:1-7). Theologically it is the church's nature and function that figure prominently throughout the section. The church is presented as a community of sharing, empowered by the Spirit for witness and healing, and as the continuation of Jesus' ministry.

The Pentecost passage itself (the target circle of our example) provides the crucial empowerment by the Spirit that gives birth to the church's character. The disciples obey Jesus' command to remain in Jerusalem (1:4), and there their Lord's promise of power (1:8) is fulfilled when they are baptized with the Spirit (1:5). With the gift of that "power from on high" (Luke 24:49) the church is enabled to fulfill Jesus' promise that they would be his witnesses in Jerusalem and Judea (1:8).

In this case, the theme of the passage fits perfectly with the larger context of the whole book of Acts and the subunit 1:15—8:3. The passage looks different to us, thanks to seeing it in its literary context. But now we must do more.

Discern the Text's Theological Themes

With the passage now focused in its wider setting, we can move on to the second major division in the process, namely, the specific theological themes in the text itself. We move from context to text.

The text's own words. The initial stage of theological inquiry of the text itself naturally involves seeing clearly the sense of its own words. We must attend to details of its expressions—specific words, phrases, and their sequence. Suppose, for instance, that it is the Sunday of the Resurrection of Our Lord (Series B), and our text is 1 Corinthians 15:1-11. Beginning in verse 4 we notice the repetition of the word *that* (*hoti* in Greek) and the fact that in each case it introduces an affirmation about Christ: "that Christ died for our sins . . . that he was buried . . . that he was raised on the third day . . . and that he appeared to Cephas . . ." (vv. 4-5). We are dealing with an early creed quoted by Paul, and *that* introduces discrete affirmations.

The text's structure. But the literary structure (flow or movement) and other literary features (for example, irony and allusions to other passages) are equally important for theological meaning. Sometimes, for instance, the way a theme is framed in the movement of the passage indicates its importance. First Corinthians 15 begins with Paul's reminding the readers of the gospel message he preached among them. Later, verses 12 and 13 (beginning the second lesson for Epiphany 6, C) are a kind of pivot in the argument of 1 Corinthians 15. Here the text shifts attention from Christ's resurrection to the believers' resurrection, which then becomes the key theme of the chapter. The movement of the passage gives us clues to the role of a theological idea in any given passage.

The movement of which we speak may be of several kinds, depending on the genre of the literature under investigation. In a narrative text *movement in the plot* interests us. For instance, in 2 Samuel 12:1-15 David's repentance constitutes the climax of the story, only after Nathan has declared, "You are the man!" Movement in narrative passages has to do simply with the order in which events are told. In some non-narrative passages (such as 1 Cor. 15) we are looking for *logical or rational movement* in thought. It may be in the order of the evidence or the conclusion of an argument. For an example see the reference to 1 Corinthians 15:12-13 above. *Poetic or liturgical movement* is still another structure. These are developments in the text that are more emotive than logical; they are shifts in mood. In Psalm 51, for instance, there is a turn at verse 15, after the confessional portion of the psalm, and attention is focused on praise and sacrifice in verses 16-19.

Discerning the movement of a passage enables us to see the epicenter of the reading, and it is there that we gain a clue to the theology of the text. But preachers want to look particularly at the movement of the text for still another reason. The movement of the text may give us insight into what might be the movement of the sermon.[7]

Questioning the text. After getting a sense of the passage's language and movement, we ask simply, what appears most immediately about the theology of a passage? Sometimes the theological emphasis is so close it could bite us, and we need look no further. But often it will play hide and seek with us. In that case, and most often, we will need to ask a series of doctrinal questions of the text. Here we admittedly ask questions out of *our own* theological constructions. Our questions are most likely to hold our own presuppositions about the text. But having done our contextual investigation first, we are more likely to be tuned into the same frequency as the text.

When we are on the same frequency with the text, five questions are useful. What does the text say, if anything, about:

1. Human nature and the human condition?
2. Sin and evil?
3. God and God's activity, past, present, and future? (Specific forms of divine activity, such as creation, judgment, redemption, and promise.)

4. The role of agents in God's work? (Including christological questions.)

5. Human response or the response of evil?

The answers the text gives to these questions should provide us with its major theological import and allow us to move toward a conclusion.

Summarizing the text's theology. We ought now to try to state the theological message of the text in a summary comprised of as few words as possible. We formulate our statement in the light of both of the above steps: the text in its context and the text in itself.

However, at this stage we may face at least two problems. The first is the possibility that the theology of the text itself is incomplete or unclear. The text may suggest or hint at a theological idea but in itself be unclear or fail to deal with enough of the substance of an idea. We may need to ask, are the theological themes of the passage incomplete without reference to what we find elsewhere in the document? If the answer is yes, we need to bring another passage to bear on the interpretation of the one we intend to preach. We use other texts to enlighten our primary passage. After all, every pericope was written to take its place in the whole document as a singular part—not the whole—of the book's message.

A case in point is the stilling of the storm in Mark 4:35-41 (not included in the Revised Common Lectionary). The passage concludes with the disciples' question, "Who is this?" which drives the reader to the gospel's conclusion. Markan christology is incomplete without reference to the cross, and the disciples' question is never answered until the centurion makes his confession in 15:39. So, the preacher may need to invoke that climax to preach the christology of the story of the stilling of the storm.

But we may encounter a far more serious problem in trying to summarize the theology of a passage. What if the theology of the text is not sound? Of course, some would argue that biblical theology is always sound theology. But many others will agree with us that there are texts which—in and of themselves—simply offer us faulty theology. Our suggestion is that, when preaching for theological formation, we exercise freedom in using other texts or themes to correct or to frame the chosen text. The text may be used, for instance, to state only one dimension of a theological theme, and we will need to bring other dimensions alongside the text. Or perhaps it represents one of several different biblical voices on a subject (for example, human suffering), and we must put it in dialogue with other canonical voices. The preacher may use the text but then set it in a wider canonical framework to see its relationship with more prominent biblical themes. (See chapter 6 on sermon design.)

Psalm 112:1-10 (the Fifth Sunday, Epiphany, A), for instance, teaches that righteous people are rewarded with material wealth (v. 3), are firm, secure, and never afraid (vv. 7-8), and will see their triumph over the wicked (vv. 8-10). We would concede that there is a sense in which righteousness is its own reward, and the Psalm expresses that. But the text overstates the case here, at least so far as our experience is concerned. We might correct the view of the Psalm with reference to the reality of Christian suffering of which Paul speaks so often. There may be times, even, when we are called to preach *against a text*. But before resorting to that extreme, we need to explore the possibilities of employing the text as a partial and inadequate comment on a larger issue.[8]

Imagining with the Text

The process we have described is dreadfully cognitive. It nurtures a careful and faithful reading and rightly emphasizes the ideological content of a text. But getting to know another person is never a purely cognitive exercise, for it also entails emotional and imaginative sensitivity. Getting to know a text likewise involves more than a cognitive exercise in digging out information. A text creates a mood, evokes emotions, and stirs the imagination. One passage can, for instance, depress us, another stir us to action, and another anger us. This results in something like an emotional dialogue between the text's and the reader's moods. Nor is theology purely intellectual; it too triggers emotional and imaginative responses.

All of this is to say that the two first stages of the process of getting to know the text's theology need to be permeated with attention to our whole response to it, including the mood it evokes. But of central interest to us is the fact that every text excites imagination, and imagination is as much a theological medium as is the intellect. We will argue in the next chapter that theology is comprised in large part of images and metaphors, both of which are products of the imagination. Therefore, in discerning a passage's theological theme for preaching we need to allow the text to play with our imaginations.

John 3:1-17 (Trinity Sunday, B) provides an easy example. Jesus' words to the inquiring Nicodemus invite imagination. To be "born from above" or "again" (vv. 3-7) is an image of the new life Christ offers. The

Greek word *anothen* is ambiguous, and that very ambiguity excites the imagination. To be embraced by the Spirit (vv. 5-8) is to experience something like a rebirth occasioned by a transcendent reality. Even Nicodemus' stubborn attempt in verse 4 to take Jesus' words literally contributes to the stirrings of our imaginations. The homiletic theologian allows this image of rebirth to activate her or his imagination and to follow its lead. The theology of the passage is the image of rebirth itself.[9]

Other passages may not be as explicitly metaphoric as John 3 but will nonetheless fascinate the imagination. So, we look for theology not alone in concepts and ideas but also in language that hints at multiple references. That requires us to think of the text's language as pointing us toward a number of possibilities, sometimes even when its primary reference is clear. In the Gospel of Mark, Jesus' pre-Jerusalem ministry provocatively concludes with the healing of blind Bartimaeus (10:46-52) and does so immediately after the Sons of Zebedee have requested places of honor when Jesus comes into his kingdom (10:35-44). Blindness in this case hints at the disciples' failure to understand Jesus and the meaning of discipleship. Receiving sight is made possible by the passion story that is about to ensue (chapters 11–16). As Bartimaeus is given sight and empowered to follow Jesus "on the way" (11:52), so will the cross and resurrection give sight to the disciples and the readers.

Imagining with the text is allowing the language of the text to ignite possibilities. In those possibilities reside the text's theological motif. Working with the text at the levels suggested in stages one and two of the process is completed only when we also allow the text to do its work in our imaginations.

Moving Toward the Sermon

Of course, the preacher's work has only begun with the completion of this interpretative process. As homiletic interpreters our final goal in getting to know a text's theology is to preach it faithfully and effectively. There is no way a preacher can exegete a text without anticipating how it will be preached. A common suggestion used to be that we determine what the text meant and, only after that determination, ask what the text means today. But in recent years we have recognized the weakness of the then/now separation, both in sound biblical interpretation in general but especially in homiletic interpretation.

Still, the preacher is not ready to concentrate on the sermon until the exegetical process is complete. When we have completed our interrogation of the text's theological message, we need to ask some specific questions about that message and our sermon. How does this theological theme relate to the congregation, its life, and its journey?[10] How might the text's movement shape the sermon's movement? How might the text's own images replicate its message in our sermon? How we answer these questions will shape the way we begin to conceive the sermon. Our work with the text with an eye toward the sermon begins to fashion the focus and function statements for the sermon.[11]

An Example of the Use of Process

Exegetical processes always appear vague and complex in their skeletal form and are better understood when fleshed out in an example. Our example is Mark 7:31-37, the gospel lesson for the Sixteenth Sunday After Pentecost, B.

Discern the Document's Theological Motifs

First, the theological motifs of the Gospel of Mark:
1. The centrality of the cross, Christ's suffering, and the suffering of his followers.
2. The secrecy of Christ's identity posed over against clear manifestations of his identity in wondrous works, with the result that in the gospel's narrative that identity is both hidden and revealed.
3. Christ's identity as Son of God, made clear by divine and demonic professions, but on the lips of a human only at the foot of the cross.
4. The inbreaking of God's dominion (the "kingdom of God").
5. The world's (and humanity's) condition in the grips of the dominion of evil.

Second, Mark 7:31-37 in its larger context, 6:45—8:10: The larger unit is bordered on either side by a story of Jesus' wondrous act on nature— the sea walk and stilling of the storm at the beginning (6:45-52) and the feeding of the four thousand at the conclusion (8:1-10). In addition to the bookends of the nature wonders the unit is comprised of:
1. A general mention of healings (6:53-56).
2. A conflict section (7:1-23) that includes issues such as washing hands, defilement, and the handling of tradition.
3. The healing of the Syrophoenician woman (7:24-30).
4. The healing of the deaf and speechless man (7:31-37).

The unit therefore emphasizes the following:

1. Jesus exercises authority to heal and to challenge the religious establishment and its handling of tradition.
2. God's dominion overcomes natural chaos, as well as the physical and social brokenness of humanity, and does so inclusively (healings of a Greek woman and a Jewish man, plus the general healings that suggest inclusivity).
3. God's dominion reveals the dominion of evil in all of its forms, including physical and social affliction, as well as the distortions perpetrated by the religious establishment.

Third, the passage in the context of the theological motifs of the whole document and its larger literary unit: To the themes in the larger unit the passage contributes an example of the wholeness brought by the presence of God's dominion. It contributes to the theological emphases of the whole document in at least three ways:

1. The inbreaking of God's dominion with healing.
2. Christ's authority in healing (v. 37).
3. The secrecy-manifestation motif: The command to silence after the manifestation in Christ's healing act (v. 36).

Discern Specific Theological Themes in the Text Itself

The Text's Own Words

1. The human response of trust in bringing the man to Jesus and the communal nature of that trust and concern.
2. Christ's authority.
3. The astonishment of the people.

The Text's Structure

1. The contrast between the bringing of the man (v. 32) and the astonishment that Christ heals him (v. 37). The structure suggests the way in which Christ's actions exceed expectations.
2. The acts involved in the healing (vv. 33-34) provide impressive details: isolating the man from the crowd; fingers into his ears; use of spittle; touching tongue; Jesus' sigh; the command, "Be Opened!" addressed to heaven.

Questioning the Text
1. Human nature and the human condition?
   a. The devastation of affliction—deafness and speechlessness.
   b. The human yearning for healing. Fleeing to one who offers healing.
   c. The possibilities of human care exhibited in those who bring the man to Jesus.
2. Sin and evil?
   Affliction is due to evil's dominion, the absence of God's dominion. And that affliction takes some terrible forms.
3. God and God's activity, past, present, future?
   a. Divine redemption takes the form of the restoration of creation (that is, wholeness without affliction).
   b. Promises the alleviation of human affliction in the fulfillment of God's dominion.
4. The role of agents in God's work?
   a. Christ is the agent of God's dominion and actualizes its presence through his ministry.
   b. He asserts his authority in healing; he is authorized to bring God's rule.
   c. He does so in human ways (that is, the details of the healing mentioned above).
   d. So his identity as Son of God is hidden in the practice of ancient medicine (for example, spittle) and in the command to silence.
5. Human response or response of evil?
   a. The possibilities of human care and trust in Jesus represented by those who bring the man to be healed.
   b. Astonishment is the only possible response to the wondrous healing.

Summarize the Text's Theology
Christ is God's agent, hidden in the world, to restore humanity and heal its afflictions. The evidence of God's presence and power astonishes needy humanity. The theological themes are complete without reference to other Markan texts. But Christ's full identity as God's agent is known only in the cross. The text is preachable in and of itself, when seen in its context.

Imagining with the Text

The mood of the text is astonishment and excites imagination through a number of its features:

1. What happens in private with Jesus (v. 33a)?
2. Jesus' use of spittle and touch (v. 33b). What image is conjured up by these?
3. Jesus' looking toward heaven and sighing (v. 34). This act is ambiguous; what does it suggest?
4. The crowd's astonishment, including those who had brought the man to Jesus with the hope that the healing might be done. The hopeful astonished by the fulfillment of their hope.

Moving Toward the Sermon

How does the theological theme relate to the needs and concerns of the congregation? The congregation deals with human affliction and is not clear about God's relationship with the reality of such affliction. The theological theme emphasizes that God cares about such affliction, the presence of which indicates that God's dominion among us is as yet incomplete. A healing story such as this, however, is likely to raise the question of why God does not intervene now and overcome the affliction certain members of the congregation know and experience.

The sermon will move inductively and nurture the conviction that God cares about human affliction. It will address the fear that God is unrelated to physical affliction or that God does not care. The gospel is that God's dominion astonishes us with care for our whole existence. The turn in the sermon from the human condition to the good news of the gospel will follow the movement of the passage from affliction to healing. But that dominion of God is hidden among us—hidden in the worldly efforts to overcome affliction; hidden in spittle and touch; and hidden in the care that we have for one another as a community of faith, even as those who brought the man to Jesus cared about his condition. Astonishment arises from the results of such human care; human care enacts God's dominion when it duplicates God's own care in Christ. The sermon will try to image a contrast in the text between the implicit trust of those who brought the man to Jesus and their eventual astonishment at what Jesus does. We feebly trust Christ through our care for others, but are astonished at the results of our trust and care.

The theological themes of the passage that will be featured in the sermon include these: the dominion of God, God's compassionate concern for human welfare, and the hiddenness of the divine dominion in human care.

If nothing else, the application of the proposed procedure to the Markan story suggests the theological richness of a synoptic healing story. What we hope this process and its application to one text shows is how careful attention to a passage's theological themes yields possibility for preaching doctrines that are important to the formation of the community of faith. It's worth getting to know a text's theology.

An Outline of an Exegetical Method for Preaching Theological Themes

A. Discern the Document's Theological Motifs
   1. Clarify the theological motifs of the whole book in which the text is found.
   2. Clarify the leading theological motifs of the literary unit in which the text is set.
   3. Set the passage in this context:
      a. The theological motifs of the whole document and b. the theological themes in the larger literary unit of which the passage is a part.
         (1) How does it contribute to the themes in the larger unit? Or, does it? Is it unique?
         (2) How does it contribute to the theological emphases of the whole document? Or, does it? Is it unique?
         (3) What do you see in the theology of the passage in the context of the (a) larger literary unit and (b) the whole document?
B. Discern Specific Theological Themes in the Text Itself
   1. In the text's own words.
   2. In the text's structure.
   3. Questioning the text.
      What does the text say, if anything, about
         a. Human nature and the human condition?
         b. Sin and evil?
         c. God and God's activity, past, present, future?
         d. The role of agents in God's work? (Including christological questions.)
         e. Human response or response of evil?

4. Summarize the text's theology, including possible problems with the text's theology. Is it necessary to appeal to another passage to enlighten the theological themes of this one?

C. Imagining with the Text
1. What mood does the text evoke?
2. What language in the text stirs the imagination? What possibilities are ignited by its language?
3. What theology is hinted at in the text's images?

D. Moving Toward the Sermon
1. How does the theological theme relate to the needs and concerns of the congregation?
2. How might the text be preached in order to nurture theological understanding among listeners?
3. How will the text's movement and images influence the sermon?

4

Image as Insight[1]

Consider this passage from Isaiah 55:12 and allow its language to form a picture in your mind:

> For you shall go out in joy
> and be led back in peace;
> The mountains and hills before you
> shall burst into song
> And all the trees of the field
> shall clap their hands.

Imagine it—mountains and hills forming a chorus, the limbs of trees becoming clapping hands. This powerful poetic language evokes a vivid image in our minds.

Increasingly over the last fifteen years, homileticians have been in the process of discovering the importance of the preacher's imagery. That process has also produced more and more literature about the importance of imagination in shaping human consciousness.[2] The whole movement anticipates the likelihood that imagery will play an ever-increasing role in preaching during the new century.

Our purpose in this chapter is not to review all that has and could be said about imagery in preaching. We want only to suggest its work in preaching doctrine, but, in order to do that, we will need to sketch some essential elements of imagery and story and how each of them works.

Briefly stated, our thesis is that imagery, broadly understood, is potent in shaping theological frameworks in listeners' minds and, by deliberate and careful use of imagery, the preacher can form theological understanding.

Images and Stories

By imagery we mean the mental and imaginary pictures evoked in the listener by language. Any use of words that results in an imaginative sketch is imagery.[3] That broad definition means that our discussion will encompass a number of different kinds of sermonic materials, including stories.

Some images in sermons educe photographs. For example, "She cowered in the crowd, watching Jesus." The listener is invited to see a still picture of the woman with the flow of blood plotting her approach to Jesus (Mark 5:24-25). "Cowering in the crowd" might well then become an image carried on through the sermon to represent a posture toward Jesus. When used to refer to another reality, the image becomes metaphoric.

Stories, we suggest, are also images in the sense that they summon forth mental pictures. But in this case the mental picture involves temporal action—a motion picture, if you will. "Slowly, carefully she elbowed her way through the crowd, trying not to attract attention." Subsuming story under imagery runs the danger of simplifying the complexities of both. But our suggestion is that they function in similar ways and for the sake of this study may be held together.[4]

Another reason for treating imagery and story together is that they share a common function in the sermon. Whether the imaginary picture we evoke through language is a still image or a motion picture, we invite our listeners to reflect on its metaphorical quality. We appeal to metaphor whenever we request that an image or a story be considered in terms of its relation to the listeners' faith. By metaphor we mean only that the language refers to something else beyond itself. The still shot of the woman's cowering in the crowd, watching Jesus, may refer to a contemporary posture toward Jesus; the action segment of the woman's approaching Jesus from behind may refer to a way in which some of us approach him today. In both cases the image or story is used to refer not just to a historic event or a literary episode but to our lives. To ask listeners to imagine the relationship between a story or image and their lives is to ask them to make the language metaphorical. Both sermonic imagery and story then function in a similar way in that preachers employ metaphorical possibilities. We will return to these possibilities in our discussion of ambiguity below.

Images and stories have become important in preaching for many reasons—some complicated, but others simple. The simple reasons are enough for us at this point. We modern humans are visually oriented and becoming more so.[5] Not least among the forces that increase our visual sensitivities is the influence of television, which treats us night after night to a veritable feast of visual images and visually told tales.

But we also remember images and stories because they have impact on the imagination and get lodged in consciousness. Any seasoned preacher has learned that their listeners remember the sermon's illustrations long after they have forgotten its theme and text. People carry away from the sermon mental pictures evoked by the preacher's words; the propositions of the sermon are quickly jettisoned from memory. The images and stories are their key to the message of the sermon. If we want people to remember our sermons (and who does not?), and if they remember stories and images, then we need to fashion those carefully so that they carry the focus and the function of the sermon.

But the most important reason imagery has become so vital for preaching is that pictorial language engages the imagination and evokes response. Propositions appeal to the mind. Imagery appeals to the whole person—mind, emotions, and will. Moreover, verbal stories and pictures provoke imagination and hence participation in the sermon. And imagination is the key to it all.

Imagination is the means by which we grasp possibilities for our lives.[6] If you want me to change, you will need to help me imagine myself as something other than I am. You will need to evoke in my imagination an image of me as a different person. You want me to understand myself as a child of God? Help me imagine that. Human consciousness is changed through imagination. How we think of ourselves and our world are transformed only through imagination. What we are or what we become must first be imagined. If that is true, the sermon changes people when it helps the listeners imagine new possibilities for themselves.

Stories and images gain their power to shape consciousness through two fundamental features. First, they are potent because they add *particularity* to faith and life. This value is premised on a thesis: We learn through particularity more readily than through generalization (see chapter 1). The specific and concrete invite us to consider our own concrete and specific experience of reality as we live it. We draw generalizations from the particular, but our generalizations are rooted in the particular. Generalizations about life are second-level discourse; stories and images are first-level discourse. To put it simply: We live in the particularities of the world, and we learn through the particular.

The value of imagery and story in preaching is that they invite us to consider their truth for our lives. All stories and images are particular—concrete and specific, temporal and spatial—like our own world of experience. They appeal through their particular historicity as it relates to our historicity. Biblical stories and imaginative pictures, for instance, are the particularities of the Hebrew people and the first Christians. As such they suggest the way in which religious faith is known and lived in concrete historical situations. In their particularity they nudge us to consider the daily experiences of our lives.

Two examples of what we mean: The Genesis story of Abraham and Sarah depicts their struggle with disappointment about the future in their childlessness. Then they tried to appropriate a promise that they would have a child in their senior years—a promise that seemed at odds with their situation. Those particularities parallel the experience of many of us. The story models a way of dealing with the dilemma of the real over against a promise for the future that seems unreal.

In the synoptic gospels, Jesus is taken into the wilderness to be tempted. The image of the wilderness is ambiguous. Israel was tested in the wilderness, but it is there too that they encountered their God. Wilderness comes to represent both a region of encounter with evil possibilities and with God. Jesus is tempted in the wilderness but goes out into the wilderness later to pray (for example, Luke 5:16). In using the image of wilderness the preacher can evoke a concrete but imaginative landscape where we live—a landscape endlessly dangerous with temptations but equally capable of theophany.

As the second example suggests, images and stories also gain their power through *ambiguity*. When the image is ambiguous (as wilderness is) or the story ends without a clear resolution, each takes on a new dimension. The story or image has many possible and different meanings. In a metaphor there is always a sense in which the comparison both is and is not. The comparison may work through both the likenesses *and* the differences.[7] The same is true of a story that our listeners suppose has some relevance for their lives. Sometimes the dissimilarities are more important than the similarities with our experience. Take, for instance, the insulting story Jesus told about the workers in the vineyard. The injustice of paying all the workers for a full day's work, regardless of how many hours they actually labored (Matt. 20:1-16), clashes with what we usually think of as God's justice. The dissimilarity here triggers reflection. Through ambiguity the listener is engaged in the image, pondering the various possibilities it raises and wondering which is meant.

Images then employ the polyvalence of language, the richness of comparison. Consider, for example, Jesus' seemingly simple metaphor: "You are the salt of the earth" (Matt. 5:13). But the first referent of the metaphor is ambiguous. Salt suggests flavor, but salt also preserves food. Salt was used in sacrifice, but sharing salt was also a sign of fellowship. The image is ambiguous and teases the imagination.

Stories exploit the polyvalence of narrative, the richness of connections among narrated events or perhaps the absence of the telling of some key event. The rich man commends the dishonest manager (Luke 16:8), and we go scurrying back through the parable to find some reason that his actions should be commended. Or, the elder son is left standing out in the fields after his father's impassioned plea (Luke 15:32) and our imaginations begin to write the final scene. In these ways, among others, ambiguity excites imagination and empowers an image or story.

What does this have to do with preaching doctrine? While we hold that images and stories share common characteristics, we will separate them below for individual analysis. Images, we believe, are most often derived from story; for example, notice how the still picture of the woman with the flow cowering in the crowd is part of her whole story. Moreover, one can argue that images are miniature stories in themselves. Still, the discussion will deal with the two in the reverse of their theoretical order, so we may treat the simpler image before dealing with the complexities of story. In both cases, we will address the function of each for theological formation along the way. In conclusion we will offer a general assessment of their place in preaching that teaches doctrine.

Images in Preaching Doctrine

To open some avenues for the use of imagery in preaching we will first examine two types of images and how they function in theological formation. Then our discussion will entail examining the metaphorical character of theology itself. Finally, we will try to demonstrate the use of imagery in preaching doctrine through two examples.

Two Types of Images

In the articulation of theological themes, images may play two very different roles, depending on the nature of the language itself. The simplest sort of image is the *analogy*. It asks the listener to compare two realities side by side. The imaginative comparison invites one to learn something about the lesser known reality from the more familiar one. These have been called epiphors (meaning "seeing with").[8] "He was as big as a barn." The analogy is a throw-away image. The preacher uses it to make a point and then dispenses with it. Once you see the new reality (how really large this man was), the older reality may not be needed to understand the newer one. A proposition is extracted and carries the meaning of the comparison. What we often have called illustrations are of this kind.

The use of analogy in speaking of theological themes is ancient and honorable. However, analogy operates on the assumption that we want the listener to conceive a proposition. The image is used only to clarify or support a proposition. (For example, the old favorite, comparing a three-leaf clover to the Trinity.) But analogies can be provocative and helpful. A preacher once spoke of the way that depth perception was normally dependent on the functioning of the two eyes. When one of his eyes was temporarily inoperative, he lost the ability to judge distances accurately. The preacher went on to suggest that faith is essentially depth perception, requiring another eye for seeing—a useful way to elucidate the nature of faith.

But simple analogy is limited in its usefulness to form theological concepts, since analogy depends on propositional language. Another more powerful type of image is the *poetic* or *tensive metaphor*. Such a metaphor is one without which you can never fully comprehend or speak of the newer reality. Such language is sometimes called diaphoric, since one sees the new reality *through* another. Symbolic language is similar.[9] Some of the classical metaphors of Christian tradition are poetic and tensive. Jesus is the Good Shepherd. The metaphor continues to excite imagination. It spawns countless propositions, but each fails to capture all the meaning. The image of shepherd is irreplaceable and cannot be discarded in favor of a proposition, for it is part of the reality of who Jesus is. It is not a simple teaching technique to enable us once to see something about Jesus and then, having seen it, discard the image. The poetic and tensive metaphor participates in the truth it provokes.

The poetic or tensive image is best suited for preaching theology precisely because it works in the imagination; it goes on evoking different images. As Patricia Wilson-Kastner observes, "Every concrete image or event is 'open' in the sense that it is itself and what it appears to be, but it is also more."[10] Finally, something like a collage results in the listener's mind. Theological concepts, we suggest, are more akin to collages of images than to simple propositions, even though the Church has preserved its cherished doctrines most often in propositions. In the new century, however, collage theology may function far more effectively. But even if that is not the case, ownership of a theological concept results from imaginative pictures. Listeners first imagine the possibilities of a theological theme for themselves, then claim an imaginative possibility for themselves.

The Metaphorical Character of Theology

We can understand this use of images for theological concepts in a number of ways. First, the use of images that excite imagination is as old as the foundational communities of the Christian tradition. Paul is a prime example. Today Paul is often viewed as the egghead of the New Testament and is credited with (or blamed for) articulating the basic propositions of the Christian faith. But that is a reading of Paul from our side of the history of the Church. Actually, Paul's letters are filled with metaphorical expressions, each of which tried to suggest something of the nature of God's work in Christ. Justification by grace, for instance, drew on the comparison of what God had done in Christ with a forensic setting. To be acquitted in a court of law is compared with God's word in Christ (for example, Gal. 2:15-16). From the slave market of his day Paul drew language of redemption, freedom, and slavery (for example, Rom. 6:16-19; 1 Cor. 6:20; 7:23). Language of reconciliation and enmity (for example, Rom. 5:1, 10) are metaphors from warfare. Of course, family language is evident in adoption, stranger, children and heirs (for example, Rom. 8:12-17, 23; Gal. 4:4-7).[11] Paul used human experiences abbreviated in simple metaphors to communicate his theology to his first readers.

Subsequent theological interpretation of Paul, however, froze the metaphors into abstractions. The words were extracted from their field of reference, deprived of their analogical function, and made into disembodied concepts. The result was that the metaphors became ideas without necessarily having immediate reference to real life, when in fact for Paul's first readers they were embedded in actual experience. Theological interpretation has tended to kill the metaphorical quality and to raise up cold abstractions.

But, second, in recent years theology has been restored to its home in metaphor. Some have even argued that all theology is metaphorical. The only way we know to speak of the transcendent is through metaphor. Feminist theologians have helped us see that this is especially true in the language we normally use for God. The ancient Hebrews had no other choice but to anthropomorphize their Yahweh. So, they spoke of Yahweh as King, Warrior, and Lord. Even the name Father betrays its metaphorical basis.

As a result of discovering the metaphorical quality of theology, some speak of frameworks of understanding as images. The way we conceive a focus of faith (doctrine) is a mental picture. In understanding Christ's relationship with God, for instance, we postulate a child-parent relationship. In the context of that image we fashion our christological language. The image, in this case, functions as an hypothesis to be tested through use and scrutiny. New images may be offered, either to replace the old one or to supplement it. This enterprise supposes that theological thought is rooted in the imagination, and theological reflection entails imaginative exploration of images.

When we encourage the formation of theology in the laity by use of imagery, we tap into these current proposals in theological method. But we also call for a return to the metaphorical roots of theology in Scripture. Strangely enough, preaching doctrine in the twenty-first century requires the practice of an ancient time.

Two Examples of Imagery in Sermons

Within this theoretical context, we offer two examples of sermons that employ images to form theological understanding. We spare you the verbatim text of each and offer instead sketches of the sermons.

The first is a sermon based on the movie *Grand Canyon*.[12] The preacher begins by sketching the story line of the movie, which develops the image of the Grand Canyon of Nevada in terms of the social gap between two racial-economic classes in the United States. But this grand canyon is still deeper. Not only are we socially divided and alienated from one another. The canyon looms between us and what we sense might be the Creator's intent for us. Our self-understanding is divided. We stand on one rim of the canyon; on the other side is authentic life— the kind of life God wants for us. But this grand canyon is still deeper.

God is on the *other* side of the gaping crevice. We are alienated from our Creator, alienated from our true selves, and alienated from others.

But God has crossed the canyon and brought the other side to *us*. In Christ, God leaped the enormous fracture. And with that leap, God brings new relationships. Now we find the gap between our true and real selves bridged. Now we discover passages over the canyon to others. The deep, wide grand canyon has been closed in the gracious act of God in Christ.

Theologically the sermon addresses two essential doctrines collated with one another. The grand canyon image is used to picture human sin and its consequences. The bridging of the canyon offers the listeners a way of imagining God's saving act, and suggests that salvation has its consequences: right relationship with God, with ourselves, and with others. Through the image of the canyon, listeners are invited to find ways of thinking about sin and salvation.

The image of the first sermon is drawn from the media. The image of the second arises from Scripture. The sermon was delivered to an academic community at the close of the spring term in the season of Pentecost.[13] The text was John 16:7-14. In this text, as elsewhere in the Fourth Gospel, the evangelist plays on the polyvalence of the Greek word *pneuma*—spirit, wind, breath (for example, 3:7-8). The ambiguity of that word gives birth to the central image of the sermon.

"The winds of change are blowing through this place," the preacher begins. The sermon goes on to suggest all of the crucial changes about to take place in the community. Students will soon scatter—some to summer employment, others to summer sessions, and the seniors into the world to practice their vocations. Faculty also face shifts. Some of them will travel to places to do research, others will undertake new assignments. Winds of change threaten to blow us away. Change means making adjustments, meeting new challenges, and facing the unknown. The winds of change propel us into new and uncharted futures. They disrupt our lives, threaten the security of the academic community, and diminish close relationships.

The disciples too faced the winds of change: Their master had to go away. What did their futures hold? Amid the winds of change is another wind. Jesus promises another Counselor, the Holy Spirit. This new mysterious wind Jesus speaks of challenges and even threatens us. But this wind brings strength, empowerment for change, and guidance amid uncertainty. Its gusts drive us into rebirth (John 3:16-17), for in the wind Christ comes to us again.

This sermon uses the ambiguity of wind to image two theological themes. The winds of change name something of contemporary life—change and its threat to our security. Our existence is so fragile that we seek stability and resist change. But wind is also made to image the divine presence. The doctrine of the Holy Spirit is viewed through the image of wind, inviting the congregation to imagine the possibilities of divine presence, empowerment, and guidance in change.

Both of these examples illustrate the use of a carrying image, one image used throughout the entire sermon that unites its individual parts. This is, of course, only one of several kinds of uses of imagery. Equally effective is the image that functions only in one of a sermon's several movements.

Both of these examples use an image to both picture the human condition and to suggest the gospel message. We suggest that such imagery functions to accomplish another theological purpose. The gospel is found in the midst of its opposite. Both the grand canyon and the wind image our experience. But in that experience, too, we are invited to imagine the saving activity of God. One result of such imagery is to invite our hearers to seek God's presence in their experience of the unpleasant realities of life.

Stories in Preaching Doctrine

Stories can conjure those imaginative pictures that hold within themselves the essentials for theological formation. Stories may be even more powerful than images in their theological work. If that is the case, it is due in large part to the fact that stories entail temporality and action, and our listeners are conditioned to want action evoked in their minds. So, the motion picture quality of our stories may work better than still images to engage our listeners in thinking about doctrine in relation to their experience.

Our discussion of stories in preaching doctrine will move through several parts. We think it is important to begin with biblical stories, since we remain convinced that they are still the most vital for theological formation.

Biblical Story

One kind of story is the text's story. But why should we retell the text's story in the sermon, especially since the congregation has just heard it? We retell the biblical story in our sermons for a number of important reasons.

First, we need to attend to these stories because increasingly people do not know them. There is less and less exposure to these formative narratives. We can no longer assume that our congregations will be hearing familiar and beloved tales. But, if we believe that biblical stories are the essential ingredient in the formation of Christian community, we will emphasize them.

Second, and more important, we retell and preach the biblical stories because they hold the biblical faith—indeed, *they are the biblical faith.* Story is no longer viewed as the decorative icing on the cake, the substance of which is propositional statements of faith. Now we recognize that story is a means of discerning and defining our reality and that faith is more often expressed in narrative than in proposition. So, the biblical stories are in many cases the essence of the biblical faith itself. The Hebraic and early Christian view of reality found language in narrative form. As such, then, these stories are the formative power of the community of faith today. They are stories that fashion our identity as the people of God.

The text's story needs to appear as the foundation of the sermon and needs to be rehearsed in ways that facilitate a new hearing of the passage. There are a number of options for how the preacher retells the biblical story to allow the congregation to experience it in a fresh way. The difference among the options is the degree to which we try to bridge the gap between the past and the present in retelling the story.

First, we can tell the story in its own world in its own language. In doing so, we honor the power of the biblical text itself and allow it to work by a personal telling (rather than a reading). Second, we might tell the story with glimpses of our world interspersed with the biblical world. In this case the story is told with a mixture of the biblical language and contemporary language, spicing the retelling with the peculiar language and concepts of our time. For example, David has to do some damage control and develops a cover-up when Bathsheba is found to be pregnant (2 Sam. 11). The effort is to spark the intersection of the biblical world and our world and begin the listeners' process of finding themselves in the story and finding that the story has contemporary relevance.

Third, at times we may want to translate the story into our own idiom by thoroughly modernizing the biblical story. We transplant the story into the listeners' world and tell it as a contemporary story. There are some classic examples of this style, such as Archibald McLeish's drama

J.B., which retells the Job story as the story of a modern executive. Such a modernization invites the listeners to ask if this is not how the story would look in their world.

Finally, the preacher may assume the role of a character in the story and tell the story in a first-person monologue from that character's perspective. If done well, these may be engaging and powerful. But they demand much of the preacher—not least of all, keeping listeners engaged as participants and not spectators.

Our suggestion is that we should use all the options, varying the ways in which we retell the story. Still, it may be wise to ask the congregation to do more of the work. Lead them toward imagining the story in their world. But allow them to do that for themselves.

Yet not all the Bible is narrative. Story is but one genre of biblical literature among many (for example, Old Testament law and the epistles of the New Testament). However, even in these various genres the preacher may discern an implicit narrative. If story is as important as we have argued, the preacher may want to develop skills in finding the story beneath or behind the passage.

One example of implicit story will have to suffice. Psalm 73 has a narrative structure. Verse 1 is a recitation of the creed, which suggests a story's beginning with equilibrium.[14] But verses 2-12 contradict the creed in the evidence of the success of the ungodly. "They have no pain, their bodies are sound and sleek. . . ." Now the easy equilibrium is upset; a problem arises that throws the status quo into disequilibrium. Verses 13-16 suggest the dilemma of the believer. "All in vain I have kept my heart clean. . . ." The Psalmist searches for a resolution of the disturbance. In verses 17-20 the resolution is discovered in the eschatological justice of God in a liturgical setting: ". . . until I went into the sanctuary of God; then I perceived their end." In terms of narrative, the clue to the resolution of the disequilibrium is discovered, and a new equilibrium is established. The remainder of the Psalm is an affirmation of faith. The faith of the Psalmist represents the implications of the resolution.

Obviously, there is more to the Psalm than this, but this is to suggest that story may be insinuated by a passage that is not in itself a narrative. The preacher may want to uncover the story in the text and preach the passage by means of its implicit story. But a warning: This does not mean that we can unearth a story behind *every biblical text*.

However they are told, biblical stories derive some of their importance in preaching from the nature of story itself. They enflesh theology in one of its earliest forms. If the biblical stories worked to form the faith of the early church, they will continue to work today if retold with skill.

We use biblical stories in our preaching for obvious reasons. But why use other stories? What role do they play in the theological formation of the congregation?

Why Use Story?

The introductory section makes a case for the use of story as well as imagery. We use the biblical story and other stories as well because we humans structure our lives through story. The fragments of our experience are held together most often with a narrative. Our own narratives frequently develop layer upon layer, each layer widening the perspective: personal story, national stories, ethnic stories, and finally universal or cosmic stories that provide the outer structure that encompasses all the others. Story is the most common way of framing life and experience.

Stories invite us to construct imaginative possibilities. "Yes, it might be this way or that." Why did the O. J. Simpson trial intrigue America? Among the many reasons is the fact that it captured the imagination with the possibility that our heroes have fatal tragic flaws. (Shakespeare exploited the same imaginative possibility with his tragedies.) In the sermon, story implicitly asks the listeners to consider what-if questions. What if people are this way, life has this quality, things often turn out this way, or things seldom turn out this way for me? What if the basic reality of life is found in the execution of an innocent person? How does that affect and shape my personal story and the suffering I have known?

If our lives are encapsulated in stories, it follows that stories form human consciousness. But further, stories weld our lives with others who share the story or find elements of the story in their lives. That is, story shapes community consciousness. Stories are one means of effecting change in us and our listeners; they are one means of forming community.

Another important reason for preaching stories for the new century is that story may bridge the gap between literate and post-literate mentalities. If some cultural critics are correct, we are moving into a post-literate era[15] in which we form our lives from and around experiences that are increasingly oral rather than written. But the orality of the new century is distinctively different from that which preceded the printing press. The new orality is shaped by the media, most of all television, and the computer. It is a visual orality saturated with story and imagery. We are less and less finding our identity in literature and more and more finding it through experiences of this new orality. This poses a fundamental issue for a church whose basic formative source is a book.

Story may operate like a bridge between that literary source and the post-literate mentality of the next century. Story is still powerfully operative in a post-literate culture through media sources and has taken on different qualities. Since it is visual and less imaginative, more is required of oral story. It must deliberately paint visual pictures with words; it must be filled with action; it must move quickly toward resolution. If oral story can meet these requirement, it promises the possibility of transporting the resources of the faith from the written page into our listeners' consciousness. So, when we use story in the sermon we translate the visual (television and computer) or the literary (the Bible) into orality, so that our listeners can imagine the story's truth for contemporary life.

Components of Story

To be good storytellers requires that we understand what is involved in story. The ingredients of story have been analyzed in a number of different ways and with varying emphases. Our purposes are served by suggesting only six of the basic elements found in nearly every story.

The first is *plot*. Plot entails simply the temporal sequence of events and the relationship among them. The surgeons on *Chicago Hope* perform an experimental surgery without proper consent; it fails, and hospital officials call the surgeons to a meeting to censor them. The relationship between the events is clear in this case. In another story, those relationships might not be so clear. In the Elijah story in 2 Kings 18 and 19, why does Elijah become so despondent? What is it in the previous events that produces his mood on Mount Horeb? The relationship among the events is not clear, at least in a simple causal way.

So, gaps in the sequence of events may appear. Gaps are simply points at which something that seems vital to the reader or hearer is withheld. Such gaps may be an invitation to the reader or hearer of the story to imagine the possibilities of the relationship between the events in the narrative sequence. Preachers may use such gaps in their stories as a way of inviting their listeners to engage the story.

Of course, stories have *characters*. The characters perform the action of the plot or are the objects of the action. Characters are usually one of two kinds: flat or round. The round character emerges as a full person. His or her attributes, actions, motives, and emotions are portrayed in detail, so that the receiver of the story comes to know the character in a full way. In contrast little is said about flat characters. They serve some role in the story but are never the object of concentration.

Other features of story often include *suspense and surprise*. A good story holds the reader or hearer suspended in uncertainty. How will a resolution to the narrative be found, or will it? Surprise occurs when we are led to anticipate a certain event but the narrative contradicts our expectations as the plot unfolds. The success of suspense thrillers is often found in the surprise twist or the resolution at the end. Unpredictability is the first requirement of a good story.

Sometimes *irony* is a feature of story, although perhaps not as common as other features. The reader or listener knows something that the characters in the plot do not know. The gospel stories are great examples. The reader knows something about Jesus that the characters in the plot are trying to discover. Irony is common to our listeners because situation comedies on television often involve our laughing at the characters in the story as a result of their not knowing something we know.[16]

Stories have *narrators*. The narrator frames the story, often knows what characters do not know, and guides the readers or listeners. Genesis 18 is a good example of both the work of the narrator and irony. The narrator introduces the story: "The LORD appeared to Abraham . . ." The plot unfolds around three men who visit Abraham and Sarah and leave making the promise, "Your wife, Sarah, will have a son." We know that the three are God's messengers; Abraham and Sarah do not. The narrator frames the story and interprets it for the reader.

Finally, but important to the preacher, every story creates a *narrative world*. A story paints an environment in which its characters live and the plot unfolds. Events in the narrative presuppose a certain understanding of a lived world. A narrative invites the reader or listener to live for the time in its world. For example, the narrative world of *Beauty and the Beast* creates a unique world in which teapots and cups and saucers speak, sing, think, feel, have hopes and disappointments. It is a world in which a human takes the form of a beastly animal.

To appreciate a story requires that the reader accept this world—at least temporarily—as believable and enter it for a time. To do otherwise alienates the reader from the story, and all its value is lost. So, the reader of a story allows the narrative's world to form in his or her mind. A good story invariably portrays a world that in some way or another attracts the reader or hearer. Maybe it is the realistic portrayal of a world like ours;

maybe it is a make-believe world that allows us to escape the unpleasantness of the real world; maybe it is a terribly violent and tragic world in which we allow ourselves to dwell for a short time with a sense of relief that all this is happening to others and not to us.

Preachers are particularly interested in narrative worlds for several reasons. First, we want to tell stories that entice listeners so they can participate in the story. Second, preachers are interested in including listeners in narrative worlds where a deeper dimension of life can be experienced.

When we tell stories in our sermons, each of these six features needs careful attention. We recognize that we take a role as a narrator, the storyteller. How do we manage that role in ways that do not intrude on the story? Plot must equally concern us. How much do we need to say to make the plot discernible to the listeners? Do we dare to leave gaps that intrigue without alienating the hearers? Further, what characters are important? Which do we want to paint fully and which can we leave flat? We want the narrative world to be interesting and capture our listeners. We would like to avoid predictable sermonic stories and use those that nurture suspense and offer surprise. Irony would enrich our stories. But telling a story, even a good one, may not be enough.

Reflecting on the Story

If our goal is to nurture theological formation, our stories need to suggest imaginative pictures of a world in which something profound is at stake. We want our stories to offer frameworks for experience so that our listeners can imagine their own lives within the "what-if" of the story. To do that we need good stories. But we may also need more.

Our use of stories needs to model for the congregation the way in which a story invites and stimulates reflection. One of the weaknesses of storytelling in contemporary preaching may be that we have relinquished the role of reflection.[17] Maybe we have not helped congregations learn ways of thinking about a story that help them relate it to their experience. Moreover, in forming theological consciousness, listeners may need to be shown what it means to reflect on a story in terms of a theological perspective. How do I take this story away with me and let it work within my consciousness in ways that deepen my faith understanding?

Two cautionary notes are needed here. We do not mean to say that story does not carry its own importance, that it does not in and of itself transmit provocation and imaginary constructs. As Richard Jensen has so persuasively argued, the point is the story itself.[18] Reflection on story needs to be done in a way that protects the integrity of story's own power. Furthermore, reflecting on a story is not the same as telling the hearers what the story *means*. To do so violates the power of the story to mean something on its own without reducing it to some moral. Reflecting on story does not close the tale. It does not limit what the hearer can find in the story for themselves.

Rather, reflecting on a story means considering its possibilities. As preachers our comments on a story seek to model for the listeners the way in which we hope they will think about the story, replay it in their minds, weigh its relationship with their experience, even find parallels between the story and some portion of their own stories. So, we try in miniature to do just a bit of that kind of reflection in our sermon. The preacher rolls the story around, observing its implications. We may raise questions about it. We may even point to how the story intersects with our own experience. Most of all, in preaching doctrine we wonder out loud about the story's relationship to some fundamental theological theme.

In the controversial movie *Priest*, the young priest is guilty of a secret life that violates his vow of chastity. But he carefully conceals it from his congregation. Along the way, however, he struggles with another issue. In confession, a teenage girl tells him her secret. Her father regularly sexually abuses her. She refuses, however, to share this with her mother. The priest is torn. On the one hand, he wants to do something to stop the abuse. On the other hand, he is sworn to the confidentiality of the confessional. He cannot find a way out of his dilemma. Finally, the mother discovers her husband's behavior and is enraged at the priest for not intervening. The priest begs the girl's forgiveness, but to no avail.

Then his own secret life becomes public when he is arrested with his lover. Finally, he comes before the congregation and asks their forgiveness. Some get up and leave, others remain. But then it comes time to receive the eucharistic bread. All the members of the congregation line up to receive the bread from the other priest. The camera moves to a view from above, showing the young priest standing there alone and the teenage girl the only worshiper still seated. Then she leaves her pew and comes to him. They embrace, both in tears. And the movie ends.

What does this story mean about our forgiveness of one another? Does it mean that those most conscious of a need for forgiveness are best able to forgive others? Does it mean that forgiveness is formed in suffering? Or perhaps it has to do with sharing the experience of hidden secrets. It touches my own life, since I know how it feels to need someone who understands my own guilt. What do you think? What does it mean for your life?

Our reflection on a story seeks to facilitate the listeners' own reflection by opening possibilities without ever pretending to exhaust them. We explore possible implications of theological significance. By doing so, we model how our listeners might reflect on the story. But more, we hope that our reflections on a story we have told might model how listeners can reflect on their own personal stories. In our reflections we suggest that stories of real human experience imply something important about our Christian beliefs.

Reflection on story seeks always to honor the ambiguity of a story. The plot of *Priest* is ambiguous in its ending. To close that story, to say once and for all what it means, assaults the story itself. If ambiguity is important in enticing participation, we allow a story's polyvalence to perform its work in our listeners. We never quite get all its significance nailed down. By honoring the ambiguity of stories, we also honor the congregation and their role in preaching. We entrust to them the task of finding their own relationship with our story. That is to say, we practice the priesthood of all believers in preaching.

Theological Implications of a Story

Through reflecting on story, we invite our hearers to discover the story's implications for the framework of their experience. But that means we preachers need to become skillful in doing that for ourselves. A prerequisite for using story in preaching for theological formation of the laity is the preacher's own sensitivity to the deeper implications of a tale. The development of that sensitivity is not easy. It requires, first, that we continually expose ourselves to as many stories as possible. But then, second, we reflect whenever possible on the stories we encounter by discussing them with others. Discussion invariably enables us to see dimensions of a story that we had not yet discerned.

We conclude this discussion of stories in preaching doctrine with two examples of story and reflection. One is derived from a movie, the other from a personal experience. For each we offer a few reflections but invite you to critique each in terms of its implications for theology.

In the 1964 movie *The Pawnbroker*, Sol Nazerman is haunted by memories of the Holocaust and the death of his loved ones in the concentration camps in Europe. Those memories have made him an embittered man. He is cold and insensitive to others. He condemns those who pass through his shop as worthless dregs of society, refusing to care for another human being. He is immune to feelings, even the feeling of pain.

Into his life comes Oritz, an enthusiastic young man, who finally convinces Sol to give him a job in the pawn shop. Gradually, Oritz begins to chip at the surface of the wall Sol has constructed around himself. In the movie's conclusion, Oritz valiantly tries to stop a robbery of the shop but instead is killed. As the police leave and the ambulance carries off Oritz's lifeless body, Sol reenters his shop. He goes behind the counter. There sets a sharp four-inch nail secured to a base. Onto this spike the pawnbroker stabs each of his records of purchases. Slowly, deliberately, Sol places his hand over the spike and pushes it through the palm of his hand. The camera focuses on his face, filled with grimaces of excruciating pain. Sol wraps his hand with an old cloth, and the movie ends as he is walking down the dirty city street.

We cannot help but see the cross and the nails driven through Jesus' palms into the wood. We hear echoes of being crucified with Christ. And we wonder. We wonder how the pawnbroker's self-inflicted pain represents our own awakening to the pains of Christ and of the world. We wonder how another's death awakens our own pains.

The following story is the conclusion of a sermon one of us preached on Luke 7:13. The sermon has turned to the question of our source of a compassion for others.[19]

I recently saw the evidence of compassion in the lives of two lay people. (I'll not use their real names, although I doubt that they would mind.) Bill is a lay leader in the church—devoted, conscientious, always willing. But Bill is also scarred by life—hurt by a divorce, grieving the loss of his children. Dick is a thirty-year-old who faithfully comes to church with his parents. But he too is scarred—challenged by a mind that never matured beyond the age of ten. Generally people are polite with Dick. But they avoid him if they can, ignore him when they can, and often pretend they just do not see him.

One Sunday morning I watched Dick go to the Table for Communion. He crowded in next to Bill, elbowing his way past another in order to stand next to Bill. There he reached out his hand to shake Bill's hand—Dick's normal gesture of friendship. They stood there together and received the bread and wine. Two scarred, hurting humans, victims of life's difficulties.

Dick wanted to stand by Bill. Bill had been compassionate to Dick. He had reached beyond his own hurt to befriend Dick. He reached through his own pain to touch Dick's pain. He had treated Dick with respect and care, talked with him and not down to him. With Bill, Dick felt like a person, a somebody, a whole human.

From the pew I watched the two of them and wondered "*how?*" How could Bill feel and act this way? What allowed him to reach beyond his own hurt to have compassion on Dick? How was it possible? What empowered Bill to feel and act this way toward the nobody, the nonperson—toward one others ignored? Bill had his own problems. How could he have compassion on Dick? I watched them together, gathered around the Table to commune with Christ and with one another.

Then I saw it! Suspended high over the Table, hanging down almost to touch the two of them, I saw the cross, and I wondered. Was that Bill's secret? I saw the cross, and I wondered if it was the cross that empowered Bill's compassion. Is that cross the source of our compassion? Could it be Christ's own compassion that led him to the cross? Is that compassionate act where we gain our own compassion?

Conclusion

In this chapter we have sketched some of the essentials of imagery and story in preaching and have addressed their role in exciting theological reflection in listeners. Much more could be said about both story and imagery.[20] But we have suggested that their role in preaching doctrine in the new century takes on peculiar significance. The postmodern era promises to be one in which these indirect forms of communication will become the primary grounds for theological discourse. Imagery, including story, facilitates insight, and most especially theological insight. Seeing with the imagination is seeing with faith. And seeing with faith is vision through a theological lens.

In this chapter we have argued that reflection on story is essential for theological formation. But that sort of theological musing is only one kind of reflection that needs to characterize doctrinal sermons in the new century. We turn now to other moments of doctrinal contemplation necessary for such sermons.

5

Moments of Theological Reflection

For people today, one key source of information is television, and a destructive effect of television is fragmentation. Most of what we see on television comes to us piece by piece, often without logical connections. Commercial moments are a blur of images. Most thirty- and sixty-minute broadcasts are a series of emotionally charged moments rather than a connected sequence. Television series are built on a number of dramas going on simultaneously. TV news, light on analysis and heavy on image, cuts rapidly from story to story. "Film at eleven" is bait for viewers.

During commercial breaks, many viewers, including most young people, flick rapidly from channel to channel. When technology permits, viewers can open windows and watch several images simultaneously. The total effect is fragmentation.

Similarly, ours is a civilization of music whose patterns and delivery systems increase fragmentation. Rock concerts, Walkmen, and boom boxes assault our ears with sound. On television, music videos present a rapid succession of images and sounds that rarely follow linear logic.

Even some print materials contribute to fragmentation. Tabloids feature pictures, screaming headlines, and few words. In responsible news magazines, pictures and white space are beginning to overwhelm print.

Given the fragmentation of messages today, a fragmentation likely to increase in the years ahead, and given a generation whose sensorium has been affected by newer modes of communication, how can listeners receive and cultivate a faith marked by understanding? How can children in the faith "grow up in every way into him who is the head, into Christ" (Eph. 4:15)? How can believers learn to reflect theologically?

Moments of Learning

One model of communication describes reflection as the conclusion of a four-stage process. First, worshipers *select* what they regard as important information; second, they *organize* it mentally; third, they *interpret* it; and fourth, they employ it to *reflect* on their lives. Some theorists speak of these stages as if they were separate and sequential. In fact, these activities occur nearly simultaneously, overlapping and affecting each other.

Specifically, learning occurs at key moments. A widely held myth, fostered by the experience of schooling, is that people can and should learn continuously. This is not true. We learn at moments when we are interested in learning, when we desire to learn.

When the gospel lesson concludes and the congregation has seated itself for the sermon, listeners are bombarded by sounds and sights. Worship books drop into pew racks. A child cries. An usher moves to the rear. People fidget in their seats. Minds wander and return. In truth, listeners affected by fragmentation can *not* and do *not* pay attention to each word and sentence in a message.

Focusing is one means to overcome fragmentation. Without realizing it, listeners focus on certain moments when communication does occur. Why is it that some thirty-second spots or three-minute clusters of language grab and hold listeners?[1]

In this chapter, we will describe the planning of various kinds of learning moments that will enable fragmented sermon listeners to focus. For contemporary people who listen in snatches, these techniques will assist reflection. Critical to what we have called homiletic theology (chapter 2), these skills will enhance most preaching. Indeed, as the skills become second nature, they will prove useful in the teaching ministry of pastors. Clergy will find themselves reframing, labeling, defining, and asking appropriate theological questions in Bible studies and discussion groups.

A related benefit for listeners might be called *modeling*. By observing the pastor/preacher guide theological reflection, not only will listeners become more adept at following along, but some congregation members will become skilled at connecting the faith to the facts of their own lives, so that ministry in daily life is enhanced.

Moments of Speaking the Gospel Directly

It is our conviction that central to every sermon are moments of speaking the gospel directly. Gerhard O. Forde has identified a hermeneutical circle, "that is, proclamation heard and believed shapes a confession upon which one reflects in order to return to proclamation again."[2] While in real life things rarely happen in precisely the order conceived by systematic theologians, the essential rhythm of this schema is correct. The proclamation of the gospel, the present tense declaration of what God has done for humans in Jesus Christ, evokes a response of faith in some people, which, reflected upon, leads those believers back to that gathering about word and sacrament where the same good news is heard afresh.

The Grammar of Proclamation

Speaking the gospel directly is a present tense activity. The preacher is called to speak for God in the here and now. There is a place in sermons and a grammar for speaking of the mighty acts of God in the past, but this retrospective speaking of God is not what we are discussing. Speaking the gospel directly has the ring of contemporary claim.

Speaking the gospel directly employs active verbs in announcing what God is saying or doing today. Through the Word, God is daily electing individuals to be God's people, bringing these people to faith, enlivening them with the Spirit's gifts, encouraging them to endure life's trials, and giving them life. The Word of God is active.

Moments of speaking the gospel directly are first person to second person, "I" to "you" moments. Such is the grammar of the gospel announcement. Theologically, the word of address in the sermon is not different from the gospel word of the absolution ("I declare unto you the entire forgiveness of all your sins") or the gospel word of the benediction ("The Lord bless you and keep you"). Speaking the gospel directly has a clear "for you" quality.

The Style of Proclamation

Speaking the gospel directly does reference a human problem or situation. This serves to differentiate gospel speaking in sermons from proclamation captured in liturgical formulas. The promise of God for people who are anxious or disheartened is couched differently than the good news for those who are sick or dying.

Speaking the gospel directly is confident speech. The Word of the living God forgives sin, sets people free, and makes them children of God. This faith-evoking promise is spoken with assurance.

In a 1985 sermon preached at a Lenten retreat for pastors and lay professional leaders, a sermon linking Numbers 21:4-9 and John 3:14, the following moment of direct gospel speaking concluded the message.

> *"And the Lord said to Moses,*
> *'make a poisonous serpent, and set it on a pole;*
> *and everyone who is bitten*
> *shall look at it and live.'"*
> *At God's direction, there in the midst of the camp,*
> *Moses lifted up a serpent staff*
> *for the healing of the people.*
>
>   *And in this Lent,*
> *on our journey toward Good Friday and Easter,*
> *on our trek toward baptism, the water of life,*
> *God remembers the promise.*
>
>   *The promise . . .*
> *for you who are weary of the journey,*
> *for you who are sick to death of complaining people,*
> *for you who would rather not be leading at all,*
> *for you . . . the promise is life.*
> *For you, God lifts up another sign,*
> *God provides the ultimate remedy, God gives healing.*
>
>   *"As Moses lifted up the serpent in the wilderness,*
> *so must the Son of Man be lifted up,*
> *that whoever believes in him*
> *may have eternal life."*

In sum, moments of direct gospel speaking are marked by a particular grammar and style:

- Present tense
- Active verbs
- God, Christ, or the Holy Spirit as subject
- Speaking first person to second person
- Engaging a particular human problem or situation
- Speaking with confidence

Of course, Fred Craddock has assisted us to see that sometimes the gospel is overheard, heard obliquely rather than directly.[3] No matter what the preacher intends, the gospel is finally actualized at the ear and in the heart of the hearer. At any point in a particular sermon, even where God's judgment is being preached, a given worshiper may overhear good news. For example, if one felt abandoned by God, a message of God's judgment might speak obliquely of God's deep concern for the sinner and thus be heard as gospel. The Holy Spirit uses the Word to speak needed messages to human hearts.

Note also that the grammar and style of direct gospel speaking stand in striking contrast to speaking in the reflective mode, although gospel speaking evokes reflection. We turn to the grammar and style of reflection now.

Questioning Moments

Comprehension is an active process. It does not happen by simply leaving your ears open. Comprehension is less like a sponge sopping up water than it is like digging for buried treasure. One secret to comprehending something is to ask questions about it. Indeed, asking questions is an essential step in learning. Better questions evoke better answers.

In chapter 3 we spoke about interrogating the text, that is, entering into dialogue with it, so that in the encounter the original question(s) and what seemed to be the apparent meaning of the text are changed. Similarly, if the sermon is to be dialogical and lead to listener reflection, it will need to form itself as a conversation in which question and response play a key role. Questions help people to think things through.

Generally, in their relationships with parishioners, pastors learn to ask questions and to listen carefully for both gaps in information and deep concerns. With practice, clergy learn to pick up on both the thoughts and attendant feelings of members and to anticipate many of their questions. In the sermon itself, through question and response, and through an honest sharing of struggle, preachers engage listeners in conversations where feelings are touched and understandings are deepened.

"Who?" Questions

The question "Who?" provides a center for theological reflection. Sometimes, "Who?" is asked directly in the sermon. Always, as the sermon is conceived and prepared, the silent question "Who?" keeps the sermon on track. This key question has two facets.

Who is the real subject of this sermon?

In an evangelical sermon, God (Christ, or the Holy Spirit) is the primary actor, the real subject of the sermon. The preacher is called to speak for God, speaking that becomes the Word of the living God. It is the conviction of both of us that, where the Word of God is proclaimed, Christ is present bringing down (judgment) and raising up (grace). As Paul wrote, "Faith comes from what is heard, and what is heard comes by the preaching of Christ" (Rom. 10:17).

In the exegetical process and throughout the crafting of the sermon, it is important to keep asking, "*Who is the real subject of this sermon?*" If the subject is people, or some human situation, this speaking is not the gospel.

In the sermon itself, "who" questions can be used as transitions into moments of speaking the good news directly.

Whose promise can be trusted? Whose word is sure?

Who does stand by you and me in good days and bad?

Who is the one, then, for whom we wait?

"Who?" questions also evoke moments of reflection. God's presence is always partially hidden. The time of the Word, the time of preaching, is faith time. Even to faithful worshipers, empirical reality may suggest that God is absent, dead, or heartlessly silent.

And yet, it is in the baffled struggle to make sense of life that believers are reoriented, are opened to encounters with the One who died and is alive forevermore. Moments of revelation and reflection may be evoked by an overt posing of questions about God's (often unseen) activity.

Who is the congregation?

One answer is that the congregation is a gathering of *believers* about word and sacrament, people baptized into the death and resurrection of Jesus Christ, people who share a common faith. "Who?" questions posed in respect to the congregation probe the deepest issues of humankind's nature and the destiny and meaning of God's election.

Note, however, that these believers are disciples, people on a journey, people not yet mature in faith. Disciples are people whose thinking and doing, whose theological reflection and Christian living, are linked.[4] Simultaneously, they are learning to think about and live the Christian life. In sermons, asking who we are as Christians provides the preacher with an opportunity to keep people open to both fresh ideas and actions. People in process, becoming who they already are, are people for whom learning and growth are normal.

Of course, disciples committed to faith-reflection are not blank tablets upon whom the preacher will write, nor are they empty vessels into which pure doctrine will be poured. People who David Buttrick describes as "being-saved in the world,"[5] people committed to exploring the meaning of the faith for work and leisure, must be respected as journey partners with the preacher, their questions and ideas taken seriously, their insights honored even as occasionally they are refined or challenged.

"What?" Questions

The question "What?" is frequently asked directly by preachers doing homiletic theology. One response to the question "What?" is facts and information. "What?" sometimes seeks definition and explanation. Or, "what" may probe deeply in seeking to diagnose. We will speak of diagnosis now.

To what human situation is God's speech/activity a response?

Diagnosis is "a process of coming to know something through and through, so that one can get hold of it better for whatever purposes one has in mind."[6] Diagnostic skills are critical for pastor/preachers who wish to avoid sermons that merely scratch the surface. Doctors employ diagnostic skills for sizing up medical situations. Accurate diagnosis includes a variety of activities.

Diagnosis begins with *observation* and attention to detail. A recent visit to a chiropractor by a middle-aged man was motivated by a persistent ache in the lumbar region. Upon seeing the patient walk into the examining room, the doctor's first words were, "your right leg is longer than your left today." Observation is the beginning of diagnosis.

Probing questions follow. One danger for preachers is allowing the sermon to move on the surface level of symptoms. The presenting human difficulty may seem obvious, but the theologian will probe. What seems to be the problem? What precipitating cause(s) have been noted?

Of course, the theologian will need no reminding that *sin*, however described (for example, estrangement, rebellion, alienation), is the depth dimension of most human difficulties. Theological diagnosis presses to the root of the problem, to *sin*.

In a sermon preached on Isaiah 64:1-8, one of us posed a question for theological reflection. This use of "What?" did not seek facts and information; rather, it pressed the listeners (theological students) to more profound levels of understanding.

> "O that you would rend the heavens and come down,
> that the mountains would quake at your presence. . ."
>   Of course, God had done that . . .

on the night when the angel of death passed over
the Hebrew children;
God had done that . . .
on the day when the corpses of Pharaoh's soldiers
lay bloated on the shores of the sea;
God had done that . . .
when the bush burned with fire and was not consumed;
God had done that . . .
when Moses went up before the presence of God
and came down with the law in both hands;
God had done that, again and again,
and the people of Israel experienced God's presence.

So, is it any wonder that God's people today
feel the silence of God acutely?
Is it any wonder that God's silence
affects you and me profoundly?
This God of ours,
who sometimes seems to hide from us,
is no stranger.

What *does it mean in your lives and in mine when God apparently fails*
. . . to "rend the heavens and come down"?

What *does it mean when you and I come to worship and hear only the*
moaning of our own voices?

What *does it mean, at the place where God promised to appear, when*
God is nowhere to be found?

"Why?" Questions

"Why?" is the question of people who ponder and reflect. "Why?" seeks motives and reasons for actions. In sermons, "Why?" is the question of *motivation.*

On the human side, hopes, fears and needs often dictate what is heard and what is ignored. Identifying these human motivators will tend to hold interest in the message. As we have said, manifestations of *sin* such as pride, self-interest and greed are other motivators that become part of diagnosis.

For divine activity, "Why?" is frequently answered with reference to God's love and faithfulness. God's promises and God's desire to overcome separation are divine motivators frequently noted in biblical texts and characteristic of God's activity today.

In the sermon on resistance to leadership quoted earlier (p. 77), the preacher relied heavily on "why" questions to relate the Israelites' angry question of God in Numbers 21:4-9 to our own murmuring.

"And the people spoke against God and against Moses.
'Why have you brought us up out of Egypt to die in the wilderness?'"
 Outside the camp were the Edomites,
deadly desert fighters.
Inside the camp were resentment, rebellion, and snakes.
The snakes appeared suddenly with the rebellion,
as if out of nowhere,
as if sent by some hostile demon,
as if sent by God.
Many people were bitten and some of the Hebrews died.
 Impatient, fearful, panic stricken
they lashed out against God.
"Why have you brought us up . . . to die?"
Why? Why God?
Haunting questions.
Pressing questions.
Angry questions.
Prayed in the silence of empty nights.
Moaned from between parched lips.
Screamed from beds of pain and beside open graves.
Why? Why God?
Why me? I trusted you.
Why now? I'm still young.
Why here, in this God-forsaken place?

In Bernard Lonergan's monumental inquiry into the nature of human understanding, one key element is the question.

> Already we had occasion to speak of the psychological tension that had its release in the joy of discovery. It is that tension, that drive, that desire to understand, that constitutes the primordial "Why?" The drive to know, the compulsion to make sense of life, gives rise to and comes to focus in "Why?"[7]

"How?" Questions

If "Why?" is the question of those who ponder and reflect, "How?" is often the question of pragmatists and cynical thinkers. If the topic is hope, such people will wish to know how hope is born from despair. If the sermon theme is new life, these listeners will ask how it can blossom in them. If the text focuses on faith, these practical people will inquire how the promise of trust can become a reality. People who ask "How?" will not be satisfied by overly broad theological generalizations.

At first, "How?" will seem an annoying and bothersome question for preachers. Addressing "How?" in sermons requires an extra measure of homework and reflection on the preacher's part. With attention and experience, however, this will become easier.

For listeners, serious attention to "How?" will help to develop inquiring minds. Persons who ask "How?" will not be content to learn simply what the mother church teaches. Healthy curiosity may lead faith to seek understanding.

The question "How?" was raised in a recent seminary chapel sermon on Genesis 12:1-4, the call of Abraham. The human issue addressed is the difficulty of hearing and responding to God's call in our lives.

> I am always baffled
> by the seemingly effortless obedience of Abram.
> I don't know about you, but I must confess
> that God's call is sometimes resisted in my life.
> When I hear this ancient story
> I wonder about God's persuasive power.
> How *did God get Abram moving?*
> How *was this message communicated so forcefully?*
> How *did God get the old couple on the road?*

The repetition of the question insures that it will be heard. In this preacher's script, words without italics suggest vocal emphasis.

In summary, one secret to comprehension is posing appropriate questions. The questions we have discussed are not exhaustive, of course, but it is in response to such questions that moments of reflection occur.

Questions	Goals of Reflection
Who?	Reflection as *centering* experience
	God and Congregation
What?	Reflection as *description* of experience
	Symptoms and deeper causes
Why?	Reflection as *structure* for experience
	Motivations
How?	Reflection as *illuminator* of experience
	Process

Explaining Moments

In response to questions, *explanation* is a rhetorical process for helping to create understanding. Preachers often seem to assume that listeners automatically grasp biblical and theological concepts. They do not. Explaining is critical to understanding.

To explain is to make something plain or clear. Synonyms include such words as interpret, explicate, and elucidate. Explanation does not assume disagreement; it does not seek to persuade. Rather, explanation shares information in order to engender comprehension.

In recent years, preaching has attempted to rely primarily on narrative to communicate theological insights. And yet, as the rabbinical tradition knows, both story and concept, story and commentary, story and explanation are essential, or else story is apt to deepen rather than correct the problem of fragmentation. Reflection on story in sermon may take the form of explanation (see chapter 4). In the Genesis 12 sermon quoted above, the preacher used explanation as an appropriate response to the question "How?" The human issue addressed is the difficulty of hearing and responding to God's call in our lives. In particular, this "How?" was raised with seminary students, many of whom are candidates for ordained ministry. The brief explanation moves from obvious examples of God's channels of communication to parts of the process more difficult to accept.

> *Sometimes God's voice echoes in the depths of your being.*
> *Sometimes that voice speaks through the mouths of*
> *faculty members who love you and care about you.*
> *Sometimes that voice is heard through candidacy committees*
> *whose words and actions challenge and threaten.*
> *God uses both likely and unlikely channels to speak to you.*

In his famous sermon "You Are Accepted," Paul Tillich speaks about the manner in which grace is experienced. This teaching/learning moment of explanation is Tillich's response to an implicit "How?"

> *Grace strikes us when we are in great pain and restlessness. It strikes*
> *us when we walk through the dark valley of a meaningless and empty*
> *life. It strikes us when we feel that our separation is deeper than*
> *usual, because we have violated another life, a life which we loved, or*
> *from which we were estranged. It strikes us when our disgust for our*

*own being, our indifference, our weakness, our hostility, and our lack
of direction and composure have become intolerable to us.*[8]

Explaining need not be pedantic and boring, as the Tillich sermon
quoted above illustrates. During the past year, a most engaging Christmas sermon on the Lukan birth narrative took time to explain the para-
doxical nature of this event. On the one hand, the birth of Jesus was pure
grace, totally out of the ordinary, a child from the womb of a virgin. On
the other hand, the event was entirely down to earth, a teenage girl unex-
pectedly pregnant, a face-saving marriage. Clearly, God uses the ordinary to reveal the extraordinary. Theological explanation is critical if
preacher and listeners are to examine the relationship between human
experience and the gospel message.

Naming and Defining Moments

Naming is the first dimension of language, the process by which we identify and isolate significant realities. Naming is critical to effective
homiletic theology.

We live in a world of constant process; everything around us is in flux,
a flux that is apt to increase in the century ahead. "Out of this maelstrom
of happenings we abstract certain bits to attend to. We snapshot these bits
by naming them. Then we begin responding to the names as if they are the
bits we have named. The names we use tend to 'fix' that which is named."[9]

Actually, naming includes the thing named in a category of relatively
similar objects or events. Labels permit us to ignore certain differences
and to lump similar things together. If a particular object is labeled
"chalice," we respond to it as a cup for holding wine in a Christian ritual
meal rather than as a cup for morning coffee. Naming is the human
process for ordering the world.

However, if the process of naming (labeling) is to be effective, standards are required to determine when a particular reality may be
included in a category. These standards are set by definitions.

A *definition* specifies the essential qualities that something must have
to be labeled in a particular way. Definitions build agreement between
preacher and listeners as to the meaning of words, phrases, and concepts.
In concrete situations, people not only learn the *denotative* (dictionary)
meanings. They learn to associate the feelings *(connotations)* they experience in those situations with the words. *Bypassing* occurs when the

speaker assumes that listeners will assign the same meanings to terms as does the speaker. Remember, words do not have inherent meanings. Meanings are in people.

History, local culture, and feelings all influence meanings. Some words are loaded for everyone, that is, they evoke strong emotions. Therefore, if accurate communication is to occur, it is vital for the preacher to name and define terms and concepts continuously.

The preacher can no longer assume that listeners, many of whom are new Christians, either know or remember the specialized vocabulary of the faith. *Shorthand definitions*, phrases in apposition to technical terms, will reinforce meaning for some and will lay foundations for meaning in others. With practice, using shorthand definitions will become second nature.

Grace, God's forgiving love

Faith, trust in Jesus Christ

Justification, being made right with God

With no pretense to completeness, these brief definitions signal a more extended meaning.

What shorthand definitions lack in precision and detail is corrected somewhat by *oral definitions*. When a key term stands in need of clarification, the preacher focuses first on the common-sense meaning of the term (correct or incorrect) in the lexicon of the congregation. Having stated what the word does *not* mean, the preacher proceeds to say what it *is*. The rhetorical pattern of the oral definition assists listeners to both attend and comprehend.

> *Repentance, you see, is* not *simply feeling sorry.*
> *Repentance is* not *designed to embarrass us.*
> *Repentance is* not *public shaming at the hands of God.*
> *Rather,*
> *repentance is being turned in our tracks;*
> *repentance is responding to God's loving tug on our lives;*
> *repentance is God's good news.*

Remember the rule of three. In the oral medium, things sound better in threes and fives. Also, reiterative language aids both comprehension and memory.

Occasionally, a mediating set of three assists listeners to move from what something does not mean to what it does mean.

Repentance, you see, is not *simply feeling sorry.*
Repentance is not *designed to embarrass us.*
Repentance is not *public shaming at the hands of God.*
To be sure . . .
there must be a willingness to come before God;
human pride cannot be a barrier;
an honest admission of guilt is critical.
But most of all . . . repentance is God's activity;
repentance is being turned in our tracks;
repentance is responding to God's loving tug on our lives;
repentance is God's good news.

Other Moments of Reflection

We have been describing key sermonic moments with potential for theological reflection. These suggestions will prove useful to clergy who are serious about bringing doctrine alive for contemporary people, most of whom listen to sermons as they appropriate other communication, in fits and starts, in snatches.

While this chapter might be expanded threefold, it is essential to mention, however briefly, several more potential strategies for preaching doctrine.

Comparing and Contrasting

Comparison and contrast set similar/dissimilar realities over against each other. Comparison links two or more elements as, in some fashion, alike. Contrast highlights differences, for example, showing us what light is by putting it next to dark. By juxtaposing contraries sharply, theological reflection captures imagination and assists memory. In chapter 6 we will describe a sermon design rooted in juxtaposition that uses comparison and contrast.

At various moments within a sermon, it may be essential for listeners, if they are to reflect theologically, to know how some aspect of the Christian message is continuous or discontinuous with human experience. Accurate reflection does justice both to the continuity and discontinuity dimensions of the kerygma.

For example, in his most famous sermon Paul Tillich uses contrast to juxtapose a process for receiving grace that focuses on human activity with a process that is receptive to God's action.

You are accepted. You are accepted, accepted by that which is greater than you, and the name of which you do not know. Do not ask for the name now; perhaps you will find it later. Do not try to do anything now; perhaps later you will do much. Do not seek for anything; do not perform anything; do not intend anything. Simply accept the fact that you are accepted.[10]

Providing Clues for Searchers

Clarity rarely comes all at once. Faith seeks understanding a bit at a time. Thus, *clues* are essential to lead searchers along. A hint here, a glimmer there, and people seeking clarity are led forward.

Prepackaged answers do not belong to the person who receives them. People must be assisted to do some of their own thinking. Clues offered, a bread-crumb trail laid, will lead some to provisional answers, or at least to a deeper understanding of the questions. Listeners will have begun to reflect theologically.

In the Genesis 12 sermon quoted previously, the preacher sought to address the question of how God's Word comes to us. The text itself provided several clues.

> *How does God's will become clear?*
> *How does God speak today?*
> *How does God address us?*
> *   If we dig just a bit,*
> *there are* clues *in our text,*
> *not final or complete answers, but* hints,
> *and even a sense of direction.*
> *   Let us not ignore the obvious* clue.
> *Abram is depicted as a person of worship and prayer.*
> *When the journey to Canaan was completed*
> *we are told that Abram "built . . . an altar to the Lord."*
> *When the three moved again, another altar,*
> *then another and another,*
> *and each time Abram "called on the name of the Lord."*
> *   What could be more clear?*
> *God has established worship and prayer as means of getting in touch.*

Linking Examples and Illustrations to Reflection

As we employ the terms in this book, *examples* are specific instances of something. *Illustrations* are detailed examples. The difference between them is comparative length and complexity. Illustrations may be narrative in form—possessing a plot line having a beginning, middle, and ending. Brief examples seldom take narrative form.

Much has been written about the use of examples and illustrations to bring *clarity* to abstract material. More to the point in a new century will be the need to enflesh the gospel in picture language. Illustrations and examples will be part of the substance, not the decorative icing, of sermons that speak concretely and clearly (see chapter 1).

In the past twenty years, teachers of preaching have repudiated the bondage of narrative material to a didactic use. Rather than conscripting stories and images to amplify and clarify abstract material, many narrative preachers have adopted the pattern of story-reflection or image-reflection. In this way, reflection—if it appears at all—follows narrative rather than encasing it (see chapter 4).

Unfortunately, while freeing stories and images from their bondage, narrative preaching has tended to throw the baby out with the bath water. Examples and illustrations, together with abstraction, remain largely out of favor.

Yet all three tools are critical for doing homiletical theology. Indeed, "the capacity to think abstractly is the goal of cognitive development and the mark of adult mental competence."[11] The inability to deal with abstraction may be a reason for some theological ineptitude among laity, as we suggest in chapter 1. By moving up and down the cone of experience, from concrete to abstract and back again, the preacher cultivates listeners' ability to deal with abstraction. Notice in the following sermon how a narrative illustration prepares listeners for abstract reflection, which in turn leads to a series of brief examples.

> *When I hear the term* reconciliation,
> *I recall a personal story a North Carolina pastor*
> *(let's call him Dave Schmidt)*
> *shared with me several years ago.*
> *Dave's father was a small-town banker.*
> *Very proper, Mr. Schmidt wore three-piece suits,*
> *starched white shirts, and washed his hands a lot.*
> *"I'm sure he loved me,"*
> *Dave recounted, "but I didn't always feel it."*
> *After work his father would walk home from the bank,*
> *fold his jacket tenderly on the porch swing,*
> *and sit down to watch his son play in*

the big sandbox next to the house.
Mr. Schmidt seldom came off the porch to join the fun.
  Then one day, Dave was a demon around the house.
In three hours he broke his mother's favorite lamp,
spilled an entire quart of milk,
and got into a fist fight with the kid next door.
Dave knew that when his father heard of his antics
he was in trouble.
  But after receiving the bad news,
and for a reason Dave never understood at the time,
 his starched father slung his jacket over the rail,
rolled up his pant legs,
and came down to play in the sandbox with his son.
Dave's dad got filthy from head to toe.
  God did that for us in Jesus Christ.
In Christ, God came down from the porch.
In Christ, God got involved with us.
In Christ, God overcame separation,
effecting reconciliation.
  God is still doing that.
When alienated people shake hands,
when angry marriage partners kiss and make up,
when warring nations come to the table of peace,
God . . . is about the business of reconciliation.

This sermon fragment points out the interdependence of concrete and abstract material. The illustration provides a powerful picture of God-initiated reconciliation. The brief examples suggest that reconciliation among humans is also God's work.

Organizing Moments

In this chapter we have suggested that fragmented listeners tend to learn in snatches. Thus, we have offered ways for preachers to take advantage of this reality by crafting sermon bits to enable listener reflection.

Paradoxically, however, even as listeners are learning in snatches, their cognitive apparatus is hard at work seeking intelligible shape and order for diverse information and insights. Organization of discreet moments into a meaningful collage is the final step for some listeners in making theological sense of messages.

As we conclude chapter 5, we will describe several organizing moments in which preachers can assist listeners to reflect.

Organizing by Patterns

One way of assisting listeners to pull things together is to highlight *patterns* in the message. Such patterns, often theological in nature, can be boldfaced in learning moments.

Order is one way patterns are created. What comes first? What follows? When speakers call attention to important sequences, listeners are assisted to reflect upon their significance.

For example, the order of repentance followed by acceptance accords with much of human experience. People willing to say they are sorry expect, following that candor, to be accepted. It can be an insightful moment of learning to discover that the New Testament frequently reverses this sequence. In key biblical stories, our acceptance, our being found by God, in fact precedes and evokes repentance (see Luke 15).

Proximity is yet another way of organizing information. While a guidebook to a city or region will frequently divide chapters into neat categories—restaurants, hotels, stores, attractions—cities are rarely structured in that fashion. Their order is organic, not categorical or alphabetic. Reflection can be enhanced when things that belong together are underscored in learning moments.[12]

For example, the appointed lectionary reading on a given Sunday may focus exclusively on one aspect of Christian freedom, namely, *freedom from* absolute obedience to anyone but God. Nevertheless, this good news should not be proclaimed without at least a moment's reflection on its theological correlate, that the Christian is *freed for* the love of neighbor. These affirmations belong together in preaching as well as in the life of the Christian.

Restatement, Recurrence, Refrain

The meaningful repetition of key words, phrases, images, or other message parts assists listeners to organize, feel, and remember the message. Done skillfully, this technique will leave a *dominant impression* of the sermon in the minds of listeners.

On an admittedly modest level, the effect is similar to surround sound in theaters or exhibits. Restatement of images and even portions of a biblical text can have a powerful effect, similar in some ways to that of a melody line or refrain in a gospel hymn. Worshipers respond emotionally, and the recurrent words intensify sermon unity.

One way the brain organizes information is to distinguish *focus* from background. Focal points stand out from less distinct information. The principle of redundancy suggests that repeating key message parts in more ways than absolutely necessary for understanding helps to establish and sustain focus.

Occasionally a restatement will be verbatim, thus giving special emphasis to an idea. Usually the restatement will not be repetitious, like dragging a stick over a picket fence, but will seek different words to express the same thing. The final statement in a series is most effective when it is short, clear, and powerful.

In a sermon preached at the Lutheran Seminary in Philadelphia, Dr. Gardner Taylor chose his preaching text from Mark 16, the lament of the women on the first Easter morning, "Who will roll away the stone for us from the entrance to the tomb?"[13] In Dr. Taylor's skillful hand, the question of the women became both text and refrain. The stone became an image for multiple impediments to Jesus and his message. Using the refrain, "Who will roll away the stone?" Dr. Taylor built the sermon to an emotional and thematic moment of climax. The stone is rolled back. Christ is risen, and because he is, the barriers to his people, his ministry, and his message will be overcome.

David Buttrick has shown that the use of *reiterative language*, saying the same thing in several different ways, is effective in catching listener attention at the beginning of new sermon sections.[14] While such moments would be labeled correctly as poor writing, in the oral medium they are pleasing to the ear and the imagination. A similar use of reiterative language is effective in moments of restatement at or near the end of sermons.

Finally, *framing* the sermon is a particularly effective form of restatement. A sense of wholeness is brought to a sermon at its end by referring back to the key thought, image, or feeling with which it began. Such moments give listeners a feeling of completeness.

Conclusion

Throughout this book we have spoken about the challenge of fragmentation for those called to preach the good news and to cultivate in believers a faith marked by understanding. We have contended that this postmodern phenomenon will become more pronounced in the century ahead, with listener attention becoming increasingly fragmented.

One way for preachers to respond is by crafting sermons marked by moments for learning, such as those we have described in this chapter. Naming, defining, questioning, and explaining moments, among others, will assist listeners to select, interpret, and reflect upon theological messages.

At the same time, whether or not the speaker gives assistance, listeners will be attempting to discern patterns in what is said, will be using proximity to group material, and will be seeking closure. If the preacher fails to help, listeners are apt to construct messages other than the ones the preacher intended. In chapter 6 we will develop three effective models for crafting doctrinal sermons, so that, with the preacher's help, listeners will be enabled to develop collages of learning moments, to reflect, to see.

6

Scoping the Sermon:
Designs for Theological Reflection

Human beings are quite dependent upon organization. Our minds struggle to make sense of the world. As we suggested in chapter 5, when confronted with individual moments of theological reflection our internal systems seek patterns to relate the moments to each other.

Familiar or meaningful organizational patterns hold listener attention and assist memory. Sometimes listeners take things that have characteristics in common, but not everything in common, and compare and contrast them. Sometimes they ask questions, probing deeper and deeper in search of a satisfying answer. Sometimes they identify problems and seek solutions. In these and many other ways listeners strive to organize fragmented worlds.

Indeed, many of the classic sermon designs are pulpit reproductions of ways that human beings manage information and reflection. As David Buttrick asserts, "the sequence of a sermon will be influenced not only by the shape of biblical material but, crucially, by ways in which human consciousness functions."[1] Simply, sermon designs are attempts to shape theological messages the way people think.

So, there are two related goals of sermon design. The first is theological, to facilitate the experience by listeners of a word event. Sermon design functions as a servant of the Word. A second goal is to provide preacher and listeners with a continuity of thought and emotion.

In every sermon-making process the time arrives when the preacher has exegeted the text, gathered material, identified the major focus of the message and has begun to craft message parts to reinforce that central idea. At that point issues of continuity—how the message hangs together—and sequence—how the parts are ordered—come to the fore.

The three designs described below have been chosen to assist both preachers and listeners to connect when a key purpose of the sermon is theological reflection. Each one of the three patterns employs a different learning theory or theology to support it. Our combined teaching and preaching experience of over sixty years has convinced us that these models encourage and enable preachers and worshipers to reflect together about issues of faith.

Sermon designs ought to work a lot like preliminary drawings and models in the hands of a master builder. Never are they followed slavishly. Rather, the model becomes a general guide as long as it is helpful.

Kaleidoscopic Sermon Design

The kaleidoscope, a common and pleasurable viewing instrument, provides a model of sermon design that has the potential to engage listeners and stimulate both their imagination and reflection.[2]

The simple kaleidoscope is an optical instrument in which bits of glass and beads, held loosely at the end of a rotating tube, are shown in continually changing symmetrical forms. Employing two mirrors set at angles to each other, the scope causes the bits of glass to assume beautiful configurations. The key to the kaleidoscope is *juxtaposition*, that is, putting one thing next to another. Crystals next to other crystals, reflected in the two mirrors, create pleasing (or displeasing) patterns.

One sometimes sees the kaleidoscopic effect within pieces of art. In a collage the planned coincidence of various pieces of material—tissue paper, metal, glass, cloth—may create special effects.

Juxtaposition: A Method of Thinking

Day after day in this media age people are bombarded with countless bits of information from television, computers, conversation, radio, and newspapers. Sanitation workers hit the picket line; a tanker spills oil on the high seas; corrupt police stand trial; students clean up neighborhood graffiti; a mob figure is murdered. The list is endless. Yet somehow ordinary people must make sense of these fragments of information.

We suggested in chapter 5 that one way humans seek to deal with a glut of information is to place it side by side with existing data to *compare and contrast*. For example, is the walkout by city workers linked to similar problems in other cities? Are the wages and work hour changes being sought fair or outrageous? What are the pros and cons of privatizing city services? Placing things side by side, comparing and contrasting, is a key way people frame the fragments and seek to understand their world.

Sometimes, when people do place things over against each other, sparks fly. Setting things in opposition can be discomforting and, sometimes, revealing. Observing both similarities and differences, may be mind boggling.

Some human processes and theological methods are dedicated to resolving contradictions. A theology of juxtaposition, however, seeks to highlight rather than resolve tensions. Harvey Cox has written, "Juxtaposition celebrates the collision of symbol and situation as the occasion for new experience and unprecedented perception."[3]

Maximizing the creative friction between two things means highlighting those points where they contradict and challenge each other. This calculated discontinuity is at the very heart of juxtaposition.

Why highlight discontinuity? Precisely because one sinful human tendency is to impose a false sense of order where order does not exist. In the biblical witness we meet spokespeople for God who are disturbers of the peace. People like Amos and Jeremiah stand over against the culture speaking words of judgment. Jesus, in his preaching of the kingdom, used juxtaposition to crack open the symbols and images of the Judaism of his day. In the Gospel of Matthew we find this formula: "You have heard it said by men of old . . . but I say unto you" (Matt. 5:21-43).

Luther's theology of the cross was dialectical. For the reformer, there were usually two ways of looking at things that could not be reconciled rationally. Thus, Luther intentionally set both truths side by side, since one without the other was partial.

Theology has followed both Paul and Luther in its fascination with paradox. The kingdom come already but not yet, the church in but not of the world, the Christian as simultaneously justified and sinner are incongruities theologians find and highlight in the biblical witness. Paradox is juxtaposing truth statements.

Kaleidoscopic Sermon Design

The kaleidoscope, with its dynamic of juxtaposition, suggests for us a model of sermon design particularly useful in assisting listeners to take antithesis and paradox seriously while becoming imaginatively and reflectively engaged. Deep awareness often takes place at the borders between realities that are juxtaposed. One image or idea challenges another. Friction produces heat. Ideas rubbing against each other in the listener's mind fire imagination. What follows is a process for planning and scoping sermons enabling worshipers to view the world in fresh ways.

1. Preparing for Preaching

Preparing to preach in a liturgical church begins by engaging seriously the appointed lectionary readings. In this book's conclusion we will argue that engagement with the church's doctrine begins at the same place.

Identify apparent contradictions in Scripture. Where Scripture presents antitheses, the preacher will recognize the opportunity for a kaleidoscopic sermon. Many biblical proverbs are two-part sentences in which the second part expresses the reverse of the first (sometimes called antithetical parallelism).

> Proverbs 14:33 is an example of this scheme: "Wisdom abides in the mind of a person of understanding, but it is not known in the heart of fools." The rhetorical effect of this structure is to create in the reader's mind opposing yet mutually informing dramas. On stage right appear people of understanding, while simultaneously on stage left, a cast of fools appears in another scene. The mind's eye roves back and forth between the two settings, comparing and contrasting.[4]

If a sermon on this saying is to achieve the effect of the proverb it will seek to reduplicate the pattern.

Similarly, Paul employs antithesis regularly to stimulate, shock, and open eyes to clearer sight. In Galatians 6:1-10 we read: "Bear one another's burdens, and in this way you will fulfill the law of Christ" (Gal. 6:2) ... "For all must carry their own loads" (Gal. 6:5). Paradoxically, both statements are accurate, and by juxtaposing them in the sermon, worshipers may see more deeply into the challenge of the Christian life.

In Paul's letter to Rome we find a sequence of theological paradoxes. Through the trespass of Adam all died; through the grace of God in Christ all live (Rom. 5). In baptism we die with Christ even as we receive the gift of new life (Rom. 6). The law brings knowledge of sin, but believers are dead to the law (Rom. 7). Life in the flesh is set over against life in the Spirit (Rom. 8). Contrasts like these abound in Paul's writings.

Determine the basis of comparison. Before two things can be compared or contrasted it must be determined what they have in common and in what respects they differ. As the text is exegeted, ask: What elements are common to these texts, ideas or images? What is the basis of comparison or contrast?

At an early stage of preparation, it may assist the preacher to take a plain sheet of paper and draw a line from top to bottom, bisecting the sheet. If single words or ideas highlight the antitheses, write these in each column. Things held in common are written in both columns.

For example, texts appointed for the season of Advent sometimes highlight the "day of the Lord." When the Hebrew prophets evoked this image they had some assurance that the meaning was understood. On this great day, God would intervene in history, overcome Israel's enemies, and establish the line of David forever.

However, while God's intervention remained a common element, several prophets began to declare that God was coming to judge Israel. The day of the Lord would be "darkness and not light" (Amos 5:18-20). A hopeful symbol, reinterpreted as judgment, was intended to shatter perceptions and call an unfaithful people to repentance.

Thus, one might write *Day of the Lord* across the top of a sheet of paper. Having bisected the paper, in one column would be written *Light* and in the other *Darkness.*

Thought-provoking contrasts to your chosen preaching text may come from a distance, perhaps from another verse in the same chapter or from another biblical book. Ask: What else is like this in Scripture? What seems to contradict it?

Some lectionaries encourage contrast preaching by occasionally choosing first lessons that are at variance with the appointed text from one of the four gospels. Occasionally a relationship of discontinuity may reside in a Hebrew Bible concept (for example, kingdom, righteousness) that is modified or corrected in the appointed gospel pericope.

Be alert to axioms of the age. Of course, not all antitheses are found in Scripture. As you exegete a text and focus on a particular theological affirmation, be sure to ask: Does the culture *reinforce* this biblical affirmation? Is it crystallized in an axiom?

"Live one day at a time" is a proverbial saying that few exemplify but that many agree is desirable. This truism suggests a life free from undue concern about the future. Matthew agrees: "Do not worry about tomorrow, for tomorrow will bring worries of its own" (Matt. 6:34). It is clear from 6:25-34 that a lack of sinful self-concern is yoked to the good news of a life of trust in a God who provides.

However, in an age of individualism, "one day at a time" may imply a selfish and irresponsible lack of planning. And yet, setting aside worry about daily necessities ought to free believers from undue personal concern for a life of faith active in love and concern for one's neighbor.

Thus, the sermon might first link the contemporary and biblical axioms ("one day at a time" and "do not worry about tomorrow") in a positive and supportive way while, later on, stimulating reflection by identifying both inappropriate and appropriate responses to the good news of God's care.

Frequently, listeners are challenged by juxtaposing a common cultural understanding (or misunderstanding) with a biblical or theological truth. As you prepare, ask: Does the culture *challenge* this biblical truth? Is it crystallized in an axiom?

Some of the best contrast sermons take the form of rebuttals. The preacher begins with a contemporary saying accepted at face value, then suddenly juxtaposes a contrary insight from Scripture or theology.

A preacher began a recent sermon by describing a pamphlet pressed into her hand while hurrying to catch a plane.[5] In this mini comic book the life of Mr. Affluent American was played out frame by frame, beginning with red sports car and nice home but followed quickly by death and judgment. Moving from reward to retribution, the tract concluded with a graphic picture of an angel standing on the shore of a fiery sea while Mr. Affluent American flailed among the flames. Can you anticipate the caption? "Where do you want to spend eternity? It all depends on you."

The tract was forgotten until a passage from Luke 12 was read and mentally juxtaposed: "Do not be afraid, little flock, for it is your Father's good pleasure to give you the kingdom." In her sermon the fear appeal of the burning lake was set over against the assuring words of Jesus. The note of judgment was countered by a graceful invitation to live now in response to God's free gift. "It all depends on you? No, it all depends on God."

2. Plotting the Movement of the Sermon

We have spoken already about the preparation of binary sermons rooted in comparison or contrast. We have noted a number of steps in preparation. It remains for us to examine the unfolding plot line of kaleidoscopic sermons.

Normally, the plot of the kaleidoscopic sermon is comprised of two movements, frequently about equal in length. Thus, about the midpoint of the sermon, the preacher makes a sharp transition from one major line of thought to another. Having examined one side of an issue the preacher turns it over and looks at the flip side.

It is critical that the listener both hear and feel that shift. A dramatic pause, coupled with a pronounced change of vocal inflection to accompany the transition, should recapture the attention of listeners.

Where the kaleidoscopic sermon is utilized to explore and explicate biblical-theological paradoxes (for example, Christians are "in but not of" the world) it is important to keep the two major movements of thought about equal in length. Overstressing one antithesis or the other may undercut the both/and nature of the paradox and leave doubt in the minds of listeners that both are equally true.

Where the purpose of the kaleidoscopic sermon is an either/or, namely, to juxtapose the conventional wisdom of the age with the truth of the gospel, there is no necessity to give equal time and attention to each. While the cultural oppositions and religious distortions of listeners do need to be challenged—and, if possible, discredited—the preacher's chief goal is always to give gospel claims full expression.

For example, in 1 Corinthians 4:8 Paul derides members of his former mission congregation for claiming to be filled with the Spirit, wisdom, and perfect human judgment *already*. In our own day, many contemporary religious groups boast of complete wisdom and a corner on truth. They claim answers to all of life's questions. The preacher could become caught up in the polemical task of debunking these theologies of glory and give little attention to Paul's essential point, that servants of Christ do not pronounce judgment "before the Lord comes" (4:5).

The sermon may then take on the character of rebuttal, with the first movement presenting a clearly false or dangerous view of reality and the second proclaiming a spirited response to it. When this is the case, the biblical text typically initiates the second movement. Thus, the rebuttal is grounded in Scripture.

While the heart of kaleidoscopic preaching is creative tension, there are sermons where, at the end, the tension is partially resolved. Sometimes the resolution of the tension will come as a surprise to the preacher as a result of deep engagement with the Scriptures, and that resolution will be offered to the congregation as a possible way through the dilemma. This final move may be brief.

On rare occasions a contrast sermon can take on the appearance of a reversal. Instead of being marked by a dramatic shift from movement one to movement two so the contrast is highlighted in the middle of the sermon, the plot flows smoothly from beginning to end. The contrast is thus stated sharply only at the very end of the sermon. Reversal is complete when the final line of the sermon is proclaimed as the mirror image of the initial line. The plot often develops in this way:

- common axiom stated
- axiom developed, illustrated, explained
- axiom questioned (usually on the basis of the text)
- opposition developed, illustrated, explained
- contrary axiom stated

The gospel is often at odds with human experience. The good news of salvation is for sinners who frequently resist this news. Juxtaposition tells the truth by recognizing discontinuity. By juxtaposing contraries, by seeking to highlight rather than resolve tensions, the kaleidoscopic design engages listeners, captures their imaginations, and stimulates honest theological reflection.

Microscopic Sermon Design

The microscope provides us with a model of sermon design that, with careful adjustment, enables us to see deeply into life.

The use of microscopes is not restricted to serious scientists. Indeed, microscopes are common Christmas gifts for curious American youth. Tiny bits of petals and flowers are readily examined under low power. What does a spider look like up close? Quartered and mounted on a glass slide, the intricate design of the spider is revealed. Later, in science or biology classes, students have access to powerful microscopes. What does water look like beyond what the naked eye reveals? Through the lens, a droplet is seen teeming with life.

Questioning: A Method of Thinking

Because life is like that droplet of water, and because many humans are naturally curious, we seek ways to put the human condition under the lens. Lacking a mechanical instrument for doing this, questions become a way to probe, to dig deeper into the nature of things.

People learn by asking and attempting to answer questions. From kindergarten on, questions are one key means to learn.[6] At college, students form study groups to prepare for examinations. In apartments or dorms they interrogate each other about the material to be tested. Questions leading to answers that are incorrect, partial, or superficial evoke follow-up questions until some measure of clarity is achieved.

In *Thinking the Faith*, Douglas John Hall asserts that there is no "immaculate expression of the faith" that the church must "protect and preserve."[7]

> The church is summoned, always, to discover and announce for its time and place what it believes to be the "gospel." It will not be gospel if the church simply recites its accumulated dogma, whether in the form of Scripture and exegesis, historic creeds and confessions, liturgies, or systems of theology. It will be the gospel only if it is the right word, the right deed—namely, what is then and there appropriate.[8]

We are living in an age that poses penetrating questions for the church (see chapter 2). Today's congregational members seem willing to put the faith under the microscope. Moving from congregation to congregation without regard for tradition or denomination, many of today's church members bring issues that cannot be addressed in a three- or five-session membership class.

Within the past year, one pastor was asked by individuals in her Bible study group to engage a number of mind benders. They included:

What importance does the repulsive image of shedding blood, so prominent in the Bible and many of our hymns, have for my understanding of Jesus' death for sin?

Is believing the story of the empty tomb really critical to my faith?

Why does God seem so real to some people, while to others God is little more than an idea?

Sermons Shaped Like Questions

Some of the unsettling questions pastors take home from Bible studies, visits, or meetings eventually take the shape of sermons. Pastors reflect on conversations, read about issues, ponder them, pray, and by and by a text appears to illuminate the issue. Eventually, a sermon is born.

In this mode of preaching, the Word of God presents itself as *insights*, which come to the preacher in the act of preparation and engage listeners as the sermon unfolds.

> The Word is anticipated and then, within the field of that anticipation, it presents itself to the hearer. In other words, this kind of preaching *invokes* the Word, it does not *tell* it.[9]

Thinkers in the field of Christian education, particularly those relying on insight theory, offer clues for us in crafting sermons shaped like questions.[10] In Martin Luther's wrestling with a number of questions over a span of years, he experienced recurring *Anfectungen* (cognitive, emotional, and spiritual struggles) leading to creative insights. From his study of Luther and others, Robert Conrad has identified a four-stage learning process: "active struggle, passive resignation, unexpected insight, and long-range interpretation."[11]

As preachers seek to utilize creative conflict to deepen faith's understanding, this process for learning must be converted into a teaching-preaching model. The dynamics of conflict leading to insight must be scoped as an experience listener-learners can share.[12]

1. Preparing for Preaching

The normal place to begin preparation is with the Sunday readings from Scripture. This year one of us addressed the biblical question of Romans 6:2, "How can we who died to sin go on living in it?" Other Pauline questions heard frequently include:

Do you not know that you are God's temple and that God's Spirit dwells in you? (1 Cor. 3:16).

What do you have that you did not receive? (1 Cor. 4:7).

Now if Christ is proclaimed as raised from the dead, how can some of you say there is no resurrection of the dead? (1 Cor. 15:12).

However, while biblical questions naturally lead to sermons that shape themselves as questions, individual biblical questions may or may not be evocative for a particular congregation, in a specific context of ministry, at a definite time. Ask more broadly:

What questions are raised *in or by* the biblical text?

Questions troubling the lives of listeners are frequently evoked by biblical readings. For example, the oracle in Ezekiel 37 takes the form of a vision. The prophet is transported to a valley/plain teeming with bones bleached white in the sun. God asks the prophet (v. 3a), "Mortal, can these bones live?" Ezekiel defers to God who alone can bring the dead to life: "O Lord God, you know" (v. 3b). The heart of the vision is raising the dry bones by the Spirit and Word of God. People feeling personally "dry" or members of "dry bones" congregations may make the leap immediately from the Bible to today.

What contemporary human dilemma will become the catalyst for this sermon?

While meditating on the energizing of a despairing people who feel cut off from God (Israel in exile), the preacher will keep in mind the congregation who will listen to the sermon. Declining attendance, loss of lay leadership, and blunted mission may be symptoms this despairing people knows at firsthand.

What evocative question(s) can be asked about this contemporary dilemma?

Not every question will evoke the insight process. The biblical question, "Can these bones live?" will need translation into the preacher's and hearer's own context. Evocative questions arise from reflection on significant human dilemmas going on at present. The best dilemmas have characteristics of universality and ultimacy.[13]

Let us suppose that a congregation in need of revitalization has been reflecting on this. Anxious questions are being asked by members and by the church board. The alert pastor has overheard or been asked directly:

Who is responsible for this decline, and how can it be reversed?

If we try it this year, will the denomination's new evangelism program turn us around?

How can we be more hospitable to strangers, get some of them to worship regularly with us and eventually join?

Why does God permit a faithful congregation like St. Mark's to be tested in this way?

Several of these questions are marked by anger, blaming, and the search for a quick fix. Others seem to reflect a readiness to confront reality and seek long-term solutions. None picks up the good news in the text.

As the pastor prepares to preach, the biblical question "Can these bones live?" becomes "Can this declining and despairing congregation be renewed?" Even when there is *no* overt question embedded in a biblical reading, the content of the passage will frequently evoke questions and resulting insights in the mind of the preacher, questions that may have a resonance in the minds and hearts of congregants. For example, pastors and members of declining congregations will find it hard to read Revelation 3:1-2, the message to Sardis, without feeling challenged. "I know your works; you have a name of being alive, but you are dead . . . wake up and strengthen what remains and is on the point of death." The entire passage lacks an obvious interrogative, but questions are evoked.

Preachers have regularly employed rhetorical questions in sermons. Donald Baillie, the British theologian/preacher, for example, relied heavily on a format where a series of questions asked and answered shaped the evolving sermon. However, many of these questions were artificial, not authentic questions *a listener* would ask. Rhetorical questions, an excuse for sharing the preacher's own answers, are rarely evocative for worshipers.

2. Plotting the Movement of the Sermon

Consider beginning with the dilemma. While sermons shaped like questions often pose the question up front, it is sometimes more effective initially to draw listeners into the human dilemma. By bringing a human issue forcefully into the consciousness of listeners, the question eventually posed by the preacher is more likely to be owned.

In addressing Ezekiel 37, one preacher introduced the image of coma with its attendant associations of deep and prolonged sleep. How difficult it is to bring people out of a coma. The preacher introduced the recent history of his own denomination, employing statistics and quoting reflections of denominational leaders to suggest that the church body was comatose. This experienced pastor was then able to cite the congregation's own planning report to support the reality of local decline. Done in a caring way by a respected pastor, the diagnosis of coma was accepted by many people in the worshiping congregation.

Pose the focusing question. The question posed by the preacher brings the entire issue to focus and finally shapes the sermon.

> Some of you may be asking yourselves, "Can this congregation be awakened? Declining in strength and vitality, can St. Mark's be brought to life?" Let us spend some time pondering this together. "Can these bones live?"

The question itself is bracketed with interrogative language. Tone of voice, cadence, and pauses underscore the interrogative. Further, it is suggested that this be a shared question of preacher and listeners. Finally, the reiterative language signals the start of a major unit in the sermon and makes it more likely that this transition is heard by listeners.

Frequently attention to the text itself will serve to clarify or deepen the question. In Ezekiel 37 it will be insightful for listeners to realize that Israel in exile was not physically dead. Rather, the nation itself was in a kind of coma, in a state of prolonged stupor.

Sometimes, at this point of transition, prior to suggesting and assessing possible answers to the question posed, it is helpful to acknowledge briefly and, perhaps, to set aside other questions being asked.

Some of you may be asking who or what is to blame for this decline. If our building were modern, would this congregation be more attractive? If we had adequate parking, would our attendance be on the upswing? If people of German origin were still moving into this neighborhood, would St. Mark's be vital and alive? Perhaps . . . and perhaps not. Essentially, these and many similar questions are neither immediately answerable nor helpful. They have the effect of shifting blame to others. They distract us from the key question, "Can this congregation be awakened?"

Build suspense by examining possible answers. Sermons shaped like questions generally move by examining several possible answers, one after the other, until the best answer is identified. Suspense builds and listeners are prepared for whatever insights come.

Typically, the first answer is the least satisfactory. Often this is the easy answer, one that moves on the surface and comes readily to mind. This answer, with help from the preacher, is usually exposed as superficial and is readily dismissed. In our example, the one-year trial of the denomination's new evangelism program is a superficial answer. The clergy leader will surely warn the congregation against the illusion of any and all quick fixes.

In sermons shaped like questions, the second answer usually has more merit and is given, appropriately, more time and attention. Frequently, this second answer creates tension and ambiguity by risking a fresh perspective. The preacher leaves what can be seen with the naked eye and probes more deeply.

In our illustration, the second answer may reach theological issues that are beneath the question, "Why does God permit a faithful congregation like St. Mark's to be tested in this way?" Those who harbor such thoughts may feel that God is not being fair, since the wicked are prospering and the faithful are suffering. Some may be questioning God's power. How can anything happen that God does not "will"? Is it God's will that St. Mark's is in decline? Many Christians naïvely embrace a view of suffering that regards it both as God's will and as punishment for their own sin. There is evidence that Hebrews in exile shared such thoughts.

This second answer will often prepare for the third answer, the good news of the text. Frequently, the preacher will be able to seed *theological clues* that will lead, eventually, to insight and resolution for listeners.

Proclaim the best gospel answer. The final answer, the best answer available, works to resolve tension by exploring a perspective that the preacher and many listeners will find truthful and satisfying. If this final move is expected to be a moment of surprise, the sermon may end quickly to freeze the moment and attendant emotion. At other times the final answer will require interpretation. The preacher may anticipate the unspoken question, "So what; what difference does this make?" If so, further elaboration may be necessary.

In the theological tradition represented by these authors, the last and best answer of the sermon will be, as often as possible, the answer of the biblical text and will be, as often as possible, the gospel. The term *gospel* is used here both in the broad sense of God's gracious activity in the world on behalf of God's people and also in the more restricted sense of the Christ event, focusing in the death and resurrection of Jesus for the sin of the world.

Ezekiel 37 proclaims radical good news for a comatose and despairing people. No human effort will revive the nation, but God, who alone can bring the dead to life, by the Spirit and Word will create a new Israel. "I am going to open your graves, and bring you up from your graves, O my people . . . and you shall know that I am the Lord" (37:12-13).

No quick fix program of evangelism, no shallow repentance, indeed, no human effort will revive a congregation. But the God who revived Israel, the God who raised Jesus from the dead, can do this. "These bones . . . gonna walk around." This is very good news.

While the final answer is the best available, it may sometimes be partial and unsatisfying. Years ago, Professor H. Grady Davis identified a sermon design he dubbed "the question propounded."[14] The essence of this model was inquiry rather than assertion. Its method was to ask, not to tell. By refusing to propose even a partial answer, the model sought to assist listeners to raise and ponder ultimate questions. By exploring possible answers to pressing questions, concluding with the one most theologically satisfying, preachers today can do more effectively what Grady Davis sought, namely, in microscopic fashion, to enable people to look deeply at human realities that trouble and confuse Christians. Thereby, the preacher enables listeners to begin framing their experience with theological concepts and images.

Telescopic Sermon Design

A television commercial for an Acura sedan begins with a man walking deliberately across the second-floor deck of his cliff-side home. He approaches a telescope on a tripod near the rail. Peering into the scope, the viewer picks up a moving speck against the landscape. What is it?

Focusing, the speck becomes a sleek sedan racing along mountain roads. Through the telescope the automobile is seen winding in and out of sight, growing larger as it approaches. The driver, a woman, guides the Acura into our viewer's driveway. Label the picture "Homecoming."

The telescope suggests one more model for scoping the sermon, one more way of seeing. The telescope enables seeing at a distance, often allowing a journey to be viewed from start to finish. The telescope enables us to answer the question, What is that speck? Is that an automobile? Is that a robin or a bluebird? The telescope is an instrument that solves an initial problem—a problem posed *before* the scope is used.

Problem Solving: A Method of Thinking

Thinking is a complex, multifaceted human activity for making sense of things. Among the large number of ways that humans think, problem solving is absolutely basic. The term *problem solving* is often used synonymously with goal-directed thinking, because it is the kind of thinking that presses from felt difficulty toward satisfactory resolution.

Among the theological methods dedicated to resolving contradictions between faith and experience is Paul Tillich's process of correlation. While space limitations will not permit us to summarize Tillich's method adequately, in shorthand fashion, Tillich turned readily to human disciplines—including philosophy, psychology, and literature—to throw light on the human situation.[15] However, in seeking an adequate response to these human needs, Tillich turned to the gospel alone.[16] Only revelation can disclose what Tillich called "the ground of being," so only revelation can give an appropriate response to the essential human dilemma of estrangement.

For our purposes, it is sufficient to say that addressing problems raised by the culture with appropriate responses of faith, is the essential dynamic of the telescopic pattern of sermon design. We believe this practical method insures that homiletic theology will remain relevant to real human issues.

In his classic *Preaching Law and Gospel*, using both Tillich and Luther as resources, Herman G. Stuempfle Jr. develops a compatible model.[17] Stuempfle finds in Luther two complementary approaches to preaching Law. He terms these Law as "hammer of judgment" and Law as "mirror of existence." Law as mirror holds up before listeners the human condition, in order to bring them to "a heightened consciousness of the dark underside of their existence."[18]

When the good news is proclaimed, this gospel affirmation is a theological antiphon to the human dilemma. For example, if the problem identified is labeled *despair*, facing life without hope, then God's Word of promise awakens *hope*, a theological correlate of despair, an antiphon of possibility.[19] At base, a chief purpose of theology is to speak to the human dilemma. Thus, theological reflection is naturally a problem-response process.

Telescopic Sermon Design

The telescope, with its ability to track a problem from start to finish, suggests a way of scoping sermons particularly useful in assisting listeners to see more clearly both the human condition and God's antiphonal response. As we shall show, this model provides opportunity both to describe and to reflect upon God's gracious words and actions.

The use of the telescope simulates a kind of journey. The journey begins with an initial problem—a distant object whose identity is unknown. Remaining at a fixed vantage point, we travel toward the object. Coming ever closer, the problem of its identity becomes more specific. (For example, is that a duck or a goose out there?) The telescope finally allows us to view the object up close, and the problem of its identity is usually resolved.

We intend to analyze this sermon model using the metaphor of search or *journey*. Journey is a dynamic reality marked by tension and resolution. As used biblically, journey allows for the activity of God from start to finish. Listeners are fellow pilgrims from jumping off point to destination. On the way these travelers experience tension, struggle, moments of insight, God's own revelation, and the joy of arrival at journey's end.

1. Preparing for Preaching

The preacher's work begins with analysis, much of which may not find its way into the actual sermon.

Posing the problem. When a human problem or dilemma begins to appear in the exegesis of either the text or the congregation, the obvious question is, "What's the problem?" The answer is seldom obvious. In our discussion of *diagnosis* in chapter 5 it was clear that symptoms, and even the so-called presenting problem, may disguise the real problem, the theological problem. Often as part of the sermon the preacher leads the congregation through a diagnostic process, from symptoms to probing questions to clarity about the theological dilemma.

According to John Dewey (1910), one can conceive of a multistage process: (1) the recognition of a problem or difficulty; (2) the location and definition of the problem and its features; (3) the formulation of possible, alternative solutions; (4) mulling over the various possibilities to determine the most likely one; and (5) testing the selected solution. Dewey's steps confirm the need to identify the problem clearly prior to suggesting possible responses.

Begin with the terminus in mind. Most journeys have a terminus in place from the start. Implicit in the metaphor of journey is a destination, a goal, an objective toward which the traveler moves. God promised Abraham a land. Moses kept the people headed back toward that land. Jesus knew, from the Mount of Transfiguration, that he would be going up to Jerusalem.

One aspect of terminus is where the congregation will be in its *thinking and feeling* when the sermonic journey is over.[20] A second aspect of the terminus is the last major move (that is, point) that will be made in the sermon. To be sure, both are subject to mid-course correction as the sermon develops.

Return to the beginning. Every journey begins somewhere. As part of the planning process, the preacher has made some tentative decisions about the nature of the problem to be addressed. Now the question is, where is the congregation positioned in its attitudes, feelings, and understandings in respect to this particular problem or situation? In terms of the development of thought, what is the first major move to be made? Where is the jumping off place for the sermon?

2. Plotting the Movement of the Sermon

Beginning with the problem today is often the best way to engage the interest of listeners. Moving immediately to the bind people find themselves in captures attention. Then, finding a similar problem or situation in the text will demonstrate that the Scriptures are relevant to the lives of listeners (see ABBA model following).

Beginning with the problem in Scripture is helpful when the biblical narrative or image is unfamiliar and needs enlivening or explaining. Starting with the text is also useful when a surprise connection is to be made between an ancient and a twenty-first-century dilemma (see BABA model following).

If possible, the resolution to the dilemma should be found in Scripture. Having identified God's speech or action in the past (history of

Israel, life of Jesus, early church), it is important to indicate if God (Risen Christ or Holy Spirit) is still doing that. What is God's response to the human problem diagnosed?

> In Israel's characteristic pattern of speech, the address of pain to God, evokes God's powerful, intervening response. God speaks and God acts. This response of God is the second element of faithful speech that becomes an evangelical theme for the preacher.[21]

Generally the sermon moves in one of two ways, although alternatives are possible.

Problem
A Problem/situation today
B Problem/situation in the text

Response
B Response in the text
A Response today

This ABBA model has the advantages of both beginning and ending in the contemporary life of the congregation while keeping the Biblical text together at the heart of the sermon.[22] The preacher will need to be careful, however, lest this biblical section become overly long.

Problem
B Problem/situation in the text
A Problem/situation today

Response
B Response in the text
A Response today

This BABA model is a useful alternative given the circumstances noted above.

While a preacher should never become predictable in terms of how the journey is initiated, reason enough for alternative beginnings, the text and the theological problem will usually determine the best jumping off place. For example, if we are to focus the telescope on the theological dilemma of God's hiddenness, perhaps given the proximity of a deadly natural disaster (for example, hurricane), one might begin:

Problem
A God seems distant in the aftermath of a hurricane
B God seemed distant to the biblical writer (text).

If one were to begin instead with Psalm 22 on a normal Sunday, then a different treatment might be called for:

Problem

B God seemed distant to the Psalmist

A We have had similar experiences.

While most effective sermons depend upon tension and resolution, this dynamic often occurs at deep levels. It may be sensed emotionally, but it is not noted by most listeners. However, in the model we have called problem/response the dynamic is more overt.

In literature, the *crux* of a plot is the point where the action shifts, where the clue to resolution of the plot is given. This is the point in the journey where the correct route is discovered or where the traveler identifies a distant objective. Peer into the telescope; the speck enlarges and is recognized as a speeding automobile. Eugene Lowry has called this action "disclosing the clue to resolution."[23]

Clue(s), discussed briefly in chapter 5, is integral to inductive preaching. Worshipers will become as excited as preachers about scenic vistas *if* listeners are helped to experience these moments for themselves. Such moments can be intensely creative.

> The event of preaching is an event in transformed imagination. Poets, in the moment of preaching, are permitted to perceive and voice the world differently, to dare a new phrase, a new picture, a fresh juxtaposition of matters long known. Poets are authorized to invite a new conversation, with new voices sounded, new hearings possible.[24]

Conclusion

In summary, we have said that the sermon patterns discussed above enable preachers and listeners together to think about the interaction of faith and life. The kaleidoscope presents colorful and striking juxtapositions. The microscope peers beneath the surface to levels not accessible to the naked eye. The telescope enables seeing at a distance, often allowing a journey to be viewed from start to finish. If these patterns are employed by preachers over a period of time, listeners can be trained to pick up shades of doctrine, think and feel along, and do so beyond the event of preaching as theological themes both describe and interpret life.

In the final portion of this book we will speak about the cumulative effect of preaching that is self-consciously theological in content and form. We will suggest specific ways that the Word may reverberate and resound, influencing congregational life and, of primary importance, enhancing the ministry of the laity in daily life.

Conclusion

Reverberations of the Word: The Conversation Continues

A woman in a small-town church was commenting to her pastor one day about old Dr. So-and-So who had served the congregation for years and years. "He was not a terribly good preacher in any one sermon, she said, but when she stopped to think about listening to him preach week in and week out for years on end, she realized she had gotten a complete theological education without knowing it."[1]

With this anecdote we are reminded that the impact of preaching is far more subtle than the obvious content of any one sermon or series of sermons. Using the analogy of human relationships, "the quality of a relationship is not so much any one encounter as rather the accumulation over repeated interactions of almost hidden emphases, styles of thinking, attitudes, expectations, emotional responses, ways of talking or acting, and the like."[2] Similarly, assisting people to grow in their ability to reflect theologically upon life's daily challenges, including joys and sorrows, is a long-term process.

Success is dependent upon the pastor/preacher's identification of growth in the congregation's reflective ability as a key objective and then addressing it in a variety of ways over a protracted period of time. The aim is to build redundancy into the life of the congregation, so that the cumulative effect of preaching is augmented. We will contend that long-term success is more dramatic if the congregation embraces the same objective. We have spoken earlier of preaching as dialogue or conversation (chapter 1). Our concluding chapter will focus on continuing the conversation beyond the preaching of the sermon. As we suggest concrete ways the Word resounds through the life of the congregation, we will be seeking to enhance preaching's cumulative effect.

To speak about the cumulative effect of preaching, the reverberation of a full organ may be the best image. Whether one's musical preferences go to Bach or the Wesleys, nothing quite compares to the pulsing effect of a column of air in motion, resounding, echoing, surrounding.

> By "reverberation" I mean a prolonging of the sound, created through reflection or repercussion. Pushed beyond its limits, reverberation becomes echo. . . . The listener has a strange feeling of being surrounded by sound.[3]

In this postmodern era, with listener attention increasingly fragmented, it is critical that the clear note of the gospel be prolonged. This concluding chapter will speak about specific ways that a congregation can be surrounded by the sound of the Word of God, read and preached, so that it echoes in the inner self, reverberates in daily pondering and decision making, and lingers to influence serious conversation with others about life's dilemmas.

The Word Noted

When the key is pressed and the note is sounded, the note is emitted from the biblical text first. It is around the reading of Scripture and the sharing of the meal that the Christian community gathers. But the Word of God, the note sounded, is already multiple sounds, reading next to reading, text next to sermon. The conversation begins in this linkage of Scripture to Scripture and Scripture to preaching. The sound goes forth.

> The word service of Christians is both Scripture reading and preaching, juxtaposed in a lively balance, speaking together. The preaching is on the texts. It is the texts made oral, made available to us, today full of Christ in our hearing. At the same time the texts give weight and breadth to the preaching, bringing to this preaching of Christ all the biblical history and ancient apostolic authority.[4]

In many churches a unifying theme of the day is manifested in, flows through, and connects the prayer, appointed lessons, and hymn of the day. Thematic unity is pleasing to mind and spirit as well as pedagogically helpful. Redundancy, that is, providing more information in more ways than is strictly necessary to state an idea or message, will help prevent loss of information. The key is pressed, the note is sounded and begins to resound.

If it follows the reading and preaching of the Word, a theme highlighted in Scripture and sermon may reverberate in the "hymn of the day." In churches where hymns are appointed for Sundays and festivals, they should be read carefully to see if particular images or phrases offer opportunities to reinforce the message of text and sermon.

In traditions where such hymns are not suggested, pastors may wish to plan services with the sequence of lessons, sermon, hymn. A key word picture or couplet seeded in the sermon, to be discovered later as the hymn is sung, provides a delightful resonance for alert worshipers.

Most individuals learn best, or at least have learning reinforced effectively, by involvement, by activity. Participation learning is deep and lasting. Thus, while direct teaching about the use and meaning of the elements of Christian worship occurs before and after the gathering, planned or not, the lively speech and activity of worship teaches. The question is not *whether* people learn but *what* they learn as they worship. The Christian assembly becomes a school.

For example, many contemporary orders for Holy Communion contain the sequence "Christ has died; Christ is risen; Christ will come again." For worshipers this creedal formula reinforces the reality of our Lord's death as well as his victory over death. The present tense "is" affirms that the Risen One is with us. Likewise, the future "will come again" expresses the Christian hope of an eschatos.

As elements like water and wine are prepared, as objects like books and Communion vessels are handled, as sacred texts are read, as clergy and worshipers move about the space, formation happens. People grasp what this odd sharing of bread and wine means as the Eucharist is done. Bread received into hand or mouth is linked to words, "This is the body of Christ given for you." Participants grow in knowledge of the church's faith as they enact the liturgy. Reverberation becomes echo.

Where appropriate, the citation of brief portions of worship texts and actions in the sermon contributes to resonance. The quotation of words and the referencing of actions (for example, confession and forgiveness, offertory, baptism) in the sermon serve to bind the service together. Reflected upon, theological understanding is enhanced. The sound of the Word is prolonged.

The Preacher's Planning

To assist a congregation toward theological depth, the preacher's planning can begin in different places. It may be kicked off by setting goals. Sometimes it is initiated by convening a planning group. We will recommend that planning begin with analysis.

Sermon Analysis

In *Building the Word*, Randall Nichols cites a research project that suggests that we humans organize our thinking into a limited number of ideas, concepts, or themes.[5] While we seem to have an almost limitless capacity for subdivision, "it is a fact of human nature that overall we do not have more than seven, plus or minus two, truly basic ideas about the universe."[6]

It follows that an analysis of the content of a significant sample (at least six months' worth) of a preacher's sermons would identify the limited number of basic themes that preacher favors (what seminary students tend to call "my theology"). While content analysis is an exact science, one not easily mastered, even the amateur should be able to score occurrences of particular themes with sufficient accuracy to begin to expose an operative theology.

For example, following the Bible, the church affirms a variety of things about baptism, including:

- baptism is for sin
- baptism is acceptance into the body of Christ
- baptism is God's precious gift

Another six or seven biblical affirmations about baptism can be discerned directly or intuited from passages such as Romans 6:3-5. A careful reading of old sermons, noting each occurrence of a baptismal reference, should identify which themes are being stressed and which are underplayed or ignored.

When sermon analysis has been accomplished, several questions will press for immediate answers. What relation does my theology bear to the faith of the church broadly or to the distinctive affirmations of my denomination? Does my choice of themes do justice both to the center (that is, cross/resurrection) and to other important emphases of the normative Christian story? Has my theology, the treasured themes I keep repeating in endless variations, degenerated into my hobbyhorse?

The Christian year, with its focus on basic narratives and theological themes, helps the preacher avoid the worst idiosyncracies. The weekly meeting to mark the resurrection of Christ soon expanded into a weekly pattern, then a week of weeks (Easter cycle), and finally into a year of Sundays, festivals, and seasons. The first part of the year celebrates the central Christian story, pressing always toward center and goal in the Lord's passion-resurrection, while the second part of the year relates the story of the Spirit's work in forming the church.

The lectionary, which provides texts for reading in each Christian assembly, helps to ensure that the Sunday and yearly themes are echoed. At least the lectionary assures that the choice of lesson, narrative, and theme is not left to the preacher alone. No lectionary is perfect, far from it, but each has an essential scheme or organizing principle that ensures variety and a degree of congruence with the biblical witness. In a day when some churches are reducing the number and length of lessons read in the assembly, when preachers are using single-verse texts as pretexts for personal agendas, we affirm the value of a lectionary for the preacher's planning and preaching.

Congregational Analysis

Someone has said that there are at least three congregations in one: the empirical congregation, whose names appear on the official role; the worshiping congregation, people who gather regularly for Word and sacrament; and the congregation as it has been formed and shaped by the preaching, pastoral ministry, and even the personality of the clergy leader. The final two congregations are critical for purposes of analysis.

All three congregations already exist when the former pastor departs and a new pastor is called. Ernest Campbell suggested it is like being invited to join a game of pool that has already begun.[7] The balls have been racked and broken. They are all over the table and must be played where they are. How is a new pastor to determine the congregation's general level of theological knowledge and reflective ability? What dominant theological themes are shared by the worshiping congregation? Where are the gaps?

Let us assume that a pastor is beginning a new call. For analysis, the following may be suggestive. Are dominant theological themes suggested by the listing of hymns or choral music used in worship during the past year (that is, are patterns of selection evident)? Are duplicated copies or audio tapes of the former pastor's sermons available for scrutiny?

What biblical texts or hymns do congregational members request for use on Sundays or at funerals? Can the biblical/theological knowledge and reflective ability of people attending Bible study be assessed directly or indirectly? Will an adult study group agree to multiple choice test or inventory (unsigned) focusing on seminal doctrines like grace, the person of Christ, and baptism? What do members say when congregational practices are questioned (Why is that done here?)? As members begin to share more freely, are they able to reflect theologically about social, psychological, or ethical issues (for example, anger at corporate downsizing, fear of loss of work)?

To summarize, analyzing one's own preaching, while at the same time analyzing what the congregation has been hearing and internalizing, are critical planning steps for the preacher if he or she is serious about deepening over time the congregation's understanding and reflective ability.

Congregational Planning

Growth in faith's understanding will be more dramatic and lasting if the congregation itself identifies as a key objective the ability to reflect upon life's questions theologically. If meaningful conversation is to continue beyond the preaching of the sermon, from week to week, from season to season, throughout the life of the parish, careful planning is essential. Pastoral leadership is essential if such a goal is to be affirmed and taken seriously.

Proactive Planning

Proactive congregational planning has many facets. Since preaching is the major focus of this book, only a few are noted here.[8]

The *mission statement*, a concise summary of a congregation's overriding mission in its particular context of ministry, will highlight particular theological themes or code words that mark that congregation's identity. If a mission statement is to shape the self-understanding of a congregation, members will wish to engage these central themes regularly and in a variety of ways (for example, congregational study groups, a planning committee).

For example, what does it mean (as one mission statement says) that members of St. Paul's are called to "announce God's new order in the midst of the old." Where is this new order "in an empirically old-order world,"[9] one pervaded by injustice, conflict, and insecurity? What does a new order coming into being mean for people trapped in destructive political, economic, and social patterns? What does this new order mean for witness and discipleship? Preaching and teaching will need to assist worshipers to think about what the resurrection of Christ implies for people living simultaneously in Christ and in the world as a sign of God's triumph over death and decay.

Some congregations use a *values statement* to add flesh to an appropriately bare-bones mission statement. The process of brainstorming, proposing values, and selecting some from the list assists a planning committee or official board to begin to forge an identity that may distinguish a congregation from others. Such a list of values is crafted, discussed widely, and finally adopted by the entire congregation. "Attaining theological depth in the faith" might become, over time, a valued mark of a particular congregation.

While the pastoral leader of a congregation needs vision, the vision that energizes is the congregation's collective *vision* of where it is going and how it is going to get there. This vision is theological in nature. It takes roots in God's own vision for creation, witnessed to in Scripture. Clearly articulated, such a vision liberates people to be what God intended for them in a particular context of ministry. Symbolized in a formal statement crafted by a planning committee, debated, and finally adopted by the official board and congregation, the vision is a picture of the future coming into being.

Typically, the vision of the congregation takes shape in a limited number of five-year *goals*. In this age of biblical/theological illiteracy, a congregation might commit itself to become a teaching-learning center for adults. A congregation committed to an exemplary ministry of teaching could become a resource for many congregations in the area (for example, an evening school of religion, teacher training), freeing other churches to concentrate their resources in different ministries.

Realistic leaders know that goals without details go nowhere. Yearly *objectives*, proposed by a planning committee and adopted by the governing board, identify definite steps toward realizing goals and vision. For congregations weak in biblical and theological understanding, depth in the faith must be gained by concrete steps. For example: A commitment for nine months to regular theological reflection focused on the theology of work and leisure (for example, a book corner, audiotapes, an adult forum); a commitment to convene a group of eight to fifteen people who will gather weekly for nine months to deepen spiritual life through a study of the Gospel of Mark, theological reflection on concrete issues of daily life, and prayer.

In *Turn Around Strategies for the Small Church*, one strategy to bring about "conceptual and missiological renewal" is a year-long small group program designed to assist people to learn "how to study the Bible and theology together and reflect upon their own life situation."[10] James Cushman writes, "One result of the study program (Beverly Presbyterian, West Virginia) was an immediate increase in the level of commitment, interest, and participation on the part of a number of people in the church." A planned focus on the Word preached and studied causes reverberation.

Constructing a Yearly Plan

The note has been sounded. The Word has gone forth. Will it reverberate, or will the sound die in the accumulated dust under the rear pew? Can a new communalism be discovered (chapter 1)? How will the conversation continue?

Good things rarely happen overnight. If theological depth is selected as a goal, it will need to be pursued actively over at least a five-year period and probably well beyond. Joining a congregation is like jumping aboard a moving train. We become part of a journey with a before and an after. Because the congregation is on track for the long haul, while pastors and some lay people come and go, a joint commitment of both clergy and laity is essential if theological acumen is to strengthen.

Long-term commitments are addressed incrementally, with a simple plan negotiated year by year. The time of official board meetings tends to be consumed with the governance of the congregation. The same planning team that proposed a mission statement and vision, or the congregation's education committee, might be assigned responsibility to work with the pastor in proposing goals and yearly objectives.

From a communications perspective, the challenge is to build redundancy into the entire life of the congregation. In this way, preaching's cumulative effect will be enhanced. The Word will reverberate and begin to echo in the lives of members.

What theological concepts, themes, or doctrines will be highlighted in the coming year? In light of sermon and congregational analysis by the pastor, in light of congregational planning steps such as those noted above, what will be the theological foci in the coming year?

Do not attempt too much. Limit these to three or fewer. Do not ignore theological themes that are understood in a shallow manner.

What seasons, festivals, Sundays, and lectionary choices pick up the theme(s)?

The rhythm of the Christian year as reflected in the church calendar and lectionary enables the regular return to central issues of faith. The sequence of Advent, Christmas, Epiphany, Lent, Easter, and Pentecost provide specific opportunities to address human issues in light of central theological affirmations. The pastor and, perhaps, the parish worship committee can list specific Sundays and themes well in advance so musicians can select and rehearse music that is thematically harmonious.

How can the Sunday bulletin be utilized prior to preaching?

With planning, the weekly bulletin can forewarn worshipers of issues to be addressed in the sermon. Theological terms can be noted and defined. One or more of the Sunday readings can be clarified (for example, who are the Samaritans?). Questions can be posed to stir interest and create a readiness to listen and learn. Authors of hymns can be introduced and texts can be quoted and explained. With some effort, the bulletin can help to prepare the congregation for both worship and learning.

How can sermons echo following their preaching?

Where Sunday sermons are reproduced and placed in racks for members to pick up and read, the learning experience is assisted by boldfacing key definitions and insights, by appending summary sentences of content and purpose, and by suggesting questions for private or family reflection.

From among the following, what *few* tactics will be chosen each year?

Bible study. Is this the year to focus Bible study on a single book? Some groups prefer to study the appointed lessons from the lectionary, certainly an aid in making preaching dialogical conversation. Keep asking participants (and yourself) what key doctrine(s) are functioning in each lesson and how they evoke or shed light upon issues in daily life.

Sermon series. The sermon series is helpful in harnessing preaching's cumulative effects. The series can play a key role in a unified strategy to assist a congregation to add to its store of knowledge and sharpen reflection tools. Technically, a series is announced and publicized while a "course" of sermons is planned by the preacher but is not announced. Preachers committed to a lectionary can, with a little effort, craft series with integrative themes using the appointed lessons. For example, in Year C of the New Common Lectionary, Luke's lengthy travel narrative (9:51—19:27) provides a frame for a number of sayings and events on Jesus' journey to the cross, that can be linked in preaching to the cruciform journey of contemporary disciples. The theme of suffering, the theodicy question, is prominent for homiletical exploration in a Lukan Lent.

Coordinated reading program. Interested members of the congregation can be challenged to read a book that explores a theological issue or offers a Christian approach to some pressing human problem.[11] Establish a book corner or library where such material can be purchased.

Discussion group. Offer a discussion group that meets weekly during a certain period or season (for example, Advent, Lent). Discuss a novel that focuses on a theological theme. Alternately, gather a group to discuss a selected list of rental films that raise pressing human issues. Country music speaks concretely of the feelings of people in dead-end jobs, empty marriages, and various kinds of heartbreak. The songs of Willie Nelson, Dolly Parton, and others raise concerns for reflection. Use the parish newsletter to share insights from these sessions and to signal the congregation's seriousness about theological work.

Theological lexicon. Many key theological terms are understood in a surface fashion, or not at all, by contemporary worshipers. A limited lexicon of key terms—defined, explained, and illustrated from the Bible, sermons, and hymns (see chapter 5)—could be produced over a period of time by the pastor and the education committee to become a resource in the congregation's educational program. Traditional theological terms will be translated into the cultural idiom of the day. New metaphors will be discovered. Used in adult confirmation and new member instruction, the relanguaging of the tradition will take on local flavor.

Conclusion: The Conversation Continues

The initiatives noted above are suggestive. Learning and growth take place when real human issues are raised, when accepted ways of thinking are challenged, and when biblical and theological perspectives are brought to bear. As these things happen over time, Christian formation results. Believers begin to find a frame of reference for their experience. The clear note of the Word read and preached echoes and reverberates through the life of the parish. The conversation continues.

Notes

Chapter 1

1. Much of this discussion was first published in Kysar's article, "Preaching Doctrine in a Secular Culture. Losing the Theological Foliage: The Need for Renewal of Doctrinal Preaching," *Academy Accents: The Newsletter of the Academy of Preachers* (Philadelphia: The Lutheran Theological Seminary, 1993), vol. 9, no. 2, pp. 1-4.

2. Robert Bellah et al., *Habits of the Heart: Individualism and Commitment in American Life* (Berkeley: University of California Press, 1985), p. 8.

3. See this book's conclusion and the recent volumes on theology and worship, especially: Don Saliers, *Worship as Theology: Foretaste of Glory Divine* (Nashville: Abingdon Press, 1995), and Gordon Lathrop, *Holy Things: A Liturgical Theology* (Minneapolis: Fortress Press, 1993).

4. Cf. the classic of an earlier decade, Harvey Cox, *The Secular City: Secularization and Urbanization in Theological Perspective* (New York: Macmillan, 1965).

5. Bernard Brandon Scott, for instance, documents the absence of transcendence in contemporary films: ". . . no modern apocalyptic movie envisions the revelation of a transcendent reality" (*Hollywood Dreams and Biblical Stories* [Minneapolis: Fortress Press, 1994], p. 195. Cf. p. 213).

6. Cf., for example, Ward Clark Roof, *A Generation of Seekers: The Spiritual Journeys of the Baby Boom Generation* (New York: HarperCollins, 1993).

7. Scott, *Hollywood Dreams*, suggests that today "love is one of the few publicly available symbols of transcendence, of something beyond ourselves" (p. 214).

8. Cf. especially the following: Roberta Bondi, *Memories of God: Theological Reflections on a Life* (Nashville: Abingdon Press, 1994); Kathleen Norris, *Dakota: A Spiritual Geography* (Boston/New York: Houghton Mifflin, 1993); and Henri

Nouwen, *Life of the Beloved: Spiritual Living in a Secular World* (New York: Crossroads, 1996).

9. One of the most accessible discussions of postmodernism is found in Darrell Joddock, *The Church's Bible: Its Contemporary Authority* (Minneapolis: Fortress Press, 1989). Another more recent but also more complex treatment is A. K. M. Adam's volume in Guides to Biblical Scholarship: New Testament Series, *What Is Postmodern Biblical Criticism?* (Minneapolis: Fortress Press, 1995), chapter 1.

10. Adam, *What Is Postmodern Biblical Criticism?*, provides a helpful description of the "Textures of Postmodernism." He summarizes the postmodern movement with three adjectives: antifoundational, antitotalizing, and demystifying. The movement is also suspicious of all metanarratives and of the stability of any text (pp. 1–25). This summary clearly suggests postmodernism's direct challenge to both traditional religion and modern science.

11. Cf. Loren Mead, *The Once and Future Church* (Alban Institute, 1991).

12. Thomas H. Naylor, William H. Willimon, and Magdalena R. Naylor in their book *The Search for Meaning* (Nashville: Abingdon Press, 1994) speak of this fragmentation as "unconnectedness" and show how meaning is the product of the discernment of connections within a person's life experiences (for example, p. 36).

13. This is closely related to Viktor Frankl's theory of the "will to meaning." Cf. especially *Man's Search for Meaning* (New York: Washington Square Press, 1963).

14. Adam, *What Is Postmodern Biblical Criticism?*, pp. 5–16.

15. Martin Heidegger, *Being and Time* (New York: Harper and Row, 1962), p. 145.

16. Rebecca Chopp has provided both a theological discussion that relates the arenas in which this discovery was made and an important discussion of language that is relevant for preachers. Her work is also a model of postmodern theological discourse. (*The Power to Speak: Feminism, Language, God* [New York: Crossroads, 1991]).

17. Tex Sample has argued that our culture is in the midst of a transition to a new orality. *Ministry in an Oral Culture: Living with Will Rogers, Uncle Remus and Minnie Pearl* (Louisville: Westminster John Knox Press, 1994). Cf. Sample, *U.S. Lifestyles and Mainline Churches: A Key to Reaching People in the 90's* (Louisville: Westminster John Knox Press, 1990).

18. Sandra M. Schneiders, *The Revelatory Text: Interpreting the New Testament as Sacred Scripture* (San Francisco: HarperCollins, 1991), p. 126. Schneiders' discussion of tradition influenced much of what we say about the subject.

19. Ray L. Hart has called these "linguistic debris." *Unfinished Man and the Imagination: Toward an Ontology and a Rhetoric of Revelation* (New York: Seabury Press, 1979), p. 71.

20. Schneiders, *Revelatory Text*, p. 71.

21. While not addressing the postmodern world, Paul S. Fiddes explores the methodology for seeking new images for the atonement in his book, *Past Event and Present Salvation: The Christian Idea of Atonement* (Louisville: Westminster John Knox Press, 1989). For a more postmodern proposal, cf. Delores S. Williams's provocative discussion of atonement in *Sisters in the Wilderness: The Challenge of Womanist God-Talk* (Maryknoll, N.Y.: Orbis Books, 1993), especially pp. 161–67.

22. Cf. Krister Stendahl's seminal essay "Paul Among the Jews and Gentiles," *Paul*

Among the Jews and Gentiles and Other Essays (Minneapolis: Fortress Press, 1976), pp. 1–77, and Hendrikus Boers's more recent *The Justification of the Gentiles: Paul's Letters to the Galatians and Romans* (Peabody: Hendrickson Publishers, 1994).

23. Fred Craddock, *As One Without Authority* (rev. ed. Enid: Phillips University Press, 1974), and *On Overhearing the Gospel* (Nashville: Abingdon Press, 1978). Robert Stephen Reid suggests that the "new homiletic" with its emphasis on "creating an experience" actually recovered a premodern rhetorical paradigm and rejected modernist presuppositions. "Postmodernism and the Function of the New Homiletic in Post-Christendom Congregations," *Homiletic: A Review of Publications in Religious Communication*, vol. 20, no. 2 (1995), pp. 1–13.

24. Lucy Atkinson Rose, *Sharing the Word: Preaching in the Roundtable Church* (Louisville: Westminster John Knox Press, 1997), and "Conversational Preaching: A Proposal," *Journal for Preachers*, vol. 19, no. 1 (Advent, 1995), pp. 26–30. For another proposal of a different kind cf. John S. McClure, *The Roundtable Pulpit: Where Leadership and Preaching Meet* (Nashville: Abingdon Press, 1995).

25. Cf. the provocative ABC documentary *In the Name of God*, hosted by Peter Jennings.

26. Cf., especially, the work of Henry Mitchell, who has helped to relate the relevance of black preaching to contemporary trends in homiletics. *Celebration and Experience in Preaching* (Nashville: Abingdon Press, 1990) and *Black Preaching: The Recovery of a Powerful Art* (Nashville: Abingdon Press, 1991).

27. Thomas H. Troeger speaks of "A Poetics of the Pulpit for Post-Modern Times." *Intersections: Post-Critical Studies in Preaching*, edited by Richard L. Eslinger (Grand Rapids: Eerdmans, 1994), pp. 42–64.

Chapter 2

1. Gerhard O. Forde, *Theology Is for Proclamation* (Minneapolis: Fortress Press, 1990).

2. Cf. Paul Scott Wilson's discussion of homiletic theology in *The Practice of Preaching* (Nashville: Abingdon Press, 1995), pp. 71–80 and 88–96, and his definition, pp. 305–6, n. 9.

3. Cf. the helpful articles in *Concise Encyclopedia of Preaching*, William Willimon and Richard Lischer, eds. (Louisville: Westminster John Knox Press, 1995), listed under "Theology" on pp. vii–viii. For fuller discussions of theology, see Alister E. McGrath, *The Genesis of Doctrine: A Study in the Foundations of Doctrinal Criticism* (Cambridge: Blackwell, 1990); Gerhard Ebeling, *The Study of Theology* (Philadelphia: Fortress Press, 1978); and George A. Lindbeck, *The Nature of Doctrine: Religion and Theology in a Postliberal Age* (Philadelphia: Westminster Press, 1984).

4. Wilson, *Practice of Preaching*, p. 86.

5. Because of our concept of the role of experience in theology, this proposal is closer to what Ronald J. Allen understands by "revisionary theology" as opposed to "enlightenment theology." "Two Approaches to Theology and Their Implications for Preaching," *Journal for Preachers*, vol. 19, no. 3 (1995), pp. 38–48.

6. Among volumes devoted to theologies of preaching are: Richard Lischer,

A Theology of Preaching: The Dynamics of the Gospel, rev. ed. (Durham: Labyrinth, 1992); Robert W. Duke, *The Sermon as God's Word: Theologies for Preaching* (Nashville: Abingdon Press, 1960); Gustaf Wingren, *The Living Word: A Theological Study of Preaching and the Church* (Philadelphia: Muhlenberg Press, 1960); and Donald English, *An Evangelical Theology of Preaching* (Nashville: Abingdon Press, 1996).

7. David G. Buttrick writes simply, "Sermon preparation after all is nothing other than theology" (Foreword, Karl Barth, *Homiletics* [Louisville: Westminster John Knox Press, 1991], p. 10). Cf. Thomas G. Long and Edward Farley, eds., *Preaching as a Theological Task: World, Gospel, Scripture. In Honor of David Buttrick* (Louisville: Westminster John Knox Press, 1996), and Donald K. McKim, *The Bible in Theology and Preaching: How Preachers Use Scripture* (Nashville: Abingdon Press, 1994).

8. C. H. Dodd, *The Apostolic Preaching and Its Development* (London: Hodder and Stoughton, 1936).

9. Cf., for example, Iris Marion Young, *Justice and the Politics of Difference* (Princeton: Princeton University Press, 1990); Theodor Adorno, *Negative Dialectics*, E. B. Ashton, trans. (New York: Seabury Press, 1973); Elisabeth Schüssler Fiorenza, *But She Said: Feminist Practices of Biblical Interpretation* (Boston: Beacon Press, 1992), especially pp. 139–44; and Rebecca Chopp, *The Power to Speak: Feminism, Language, God* (New York: Crossroads Publishing Co., 1991).

10. Ronald J. Allen, *The Teaching Sermon* (Nashville: Abingdon Press, 1995), pp. 26–38. Allen's book is a fine treatment of the didactic possibilities of the sermon. His work differs from ours essentially in its broader scope (that is, with teaching matters other than doctrine) and its assumption of more topical preaching, where we are inclined to emphasize lectionary preaching.

11. For example, David G. Buttrick, *Preaching Jesus Christ*, Fortress Resources for Preaching (Minneapolis: Fortress Press, 1988). Cf. *The Mystery and the Passion: A Homiletical Reading of the Gospel Traditions* (Minneapolis: Fortress Press, 1992).

12. Robert G. Hughes, "Preaching as Lively Teaching," *Academy Accents. The Newsletter of the Academy of Preachers*, vol. 51, no. 4 (August 1989), p. 4. On the postmodern view of theory as ideology see A. K. M. Adam, *What is Postmodern Biblical Criticism?* Guides to Biblical Scholarship: New Testament Series (Minneapolis: Fortress Press, 1995), pp. 13–14.

13. Cf. David M. Greenhaw, "As One *with* Authority: Rehabilitating Concepts for Preaching," *Intersections: Post-Critical Studies in Preaching*, Richard L. Eslinger, ed. (Grand Rapids: Eerdmans, 1994), pp. 105–22.

14. William Muehl, *Why Preach? Why Listen?* (Philadelphia: Fortress Press, 1986), p. 16.

15. Cf. these helpful volumes: Thomas Troeger, *Imagining a Sermon* (Nashville: Abingdon Press, 1990), and *Ten Strategies for Preaching in a Multi-Media Culture* (Nashville: Abingdon Press, 1996); and Paul Scott Wilson, *Imagination of the Heart: New Understandings of Preaching* (Nashville: Abingdon Press, 1988).

16. Robert J. Schreiter, *Constructing Local Theologies* (Maryknoll, N.Y.: Orbis Books, 1985). See also Leonora Tubbs Tisdale, "Ways of Knowing and Forms of Preaching," *Journal for Preachers*, vol. 19, no. 4 (1996), pp. 30–36, and *Preaching*

as Local Theology and Folk Art, Fortress Resources for Preaching (Minneapolis: Fortress Press, 1997).

17. In the article cited above, Hughes calls this a "working theology" (p. 4).

18. Lischer, *A Theology of Preaching,* chapter 6.

19. Arthur Van Seters calls this function of homiletic theology the "declericalizing proclamation" (emphasizing the congregation's role in the process) and suggests that preachers understand doctrine in terms of "an ecclesial approach.""Dilemmas in Preaching Doctrine: Declericalizing Proclamation," *Journal for Preachers,* vol. 27, no. 3 (1994), pp. 31–40. Cf. two volumes addressed to laity concerning their role as theologians: John B. Cobb Jr., *Becoming a Thinking Christian* (Nashville: Abingdon Press, 1993), and Howard W. Stone and James O. Duke, *How to Think Theologically* (Minneapolis: Fortress Press, 1996).

20. Current homileticians who stress the role of preaching in forming Christian community include Richard Lischer, *A Theology of Preaching,* and William Willimon, *Peculiar Speech: Preaching to the Baptized* (Grand Rapids: Eerdmans, 1992), and *The Intrusive Word: Preaching to the Unbaptized* (Grand Rapids: Eerdmans, 1994).

Chapter 3

1. For descriptions of exegetical methods for preaching, cf. especially Thomas G. Long, *The Witness of Preaching* (Louisville: Westminster John Knox, 1989), chapters 3 and 4, and John H. Hayes and Carl R. Holladay, *Biblical Exegesis: A Beginner's Handbook,* rev. ed. (Louisville: Westminster John Knox, 1983). Another helpful volume is Vernon K. Robbins, *Exploring the Texture of Texts: A Guide to Socio-Rhetorical Interpretation* (Valley Forge, Pa.: Trinity Press International, 1996).

2. Cf. Rudolf Bultmann's classic essay, "Is Exegesis Without Presuppositions Possible?" *The New Testament and Mythology and Other Basic Writings,* Schubert M. Ogden, ed. (Philadelphia: Fortress Press, 1989), pp. 145–53.

3. The best example of this trend is found in the volume *The Postmodern Bible* produced by a group calling itself The Bible and Culture Collective (George Aichele et al., eds. [New Haven and London: Yale University Press, 1995]).

4. See John S. McClure's proposal for conversation with representatives of the congregation in *The Roundtable Pulpit: Where Leadership and Preaching Meet* (Nashville: Abingdon Press, 1995).

5. Also very helpful in this task are good Bible dictionaries that have articles on each individual book. See especially *The Anchor Bible Dictionary,* David Noel Freedman, ed. (New York: Doubleday, 1992), 6 volumes. *The New Interpreter's Bible,* edited by Leander E. Keck, et al. (Nashville: Abingdon Press, 1995–) includes introductory articles for each biblical book and will be available at the rate of two volumes a year over the next decade. Cf. Diane L. Jacobson and Robert Kysar, *A Beginner's Guide to the Books of the Bible* (Minneapolis: Augsburg Books, 1991,) which includes concise statements of the themes of each book.

6. See *The HarperCollins Study Bible. New Revised Standard Version,* Wayne A. Meeks, general ed. (New York/London: HarperCollins Publishers, 1993), p. 2060.

7. Paul Scott Wilson helpfully elucidates this possibility in *The Practice of Preaching* (Nashville: Abingdon Press, 1995), p. 92.

8. Wilson calls this "theological intervention" and mentions the cases in which

such action is called for: When the text has no apparent theological theme or when there is no explicit focus on either God or Christ (pp. 92–96).

9. Robert Kysar, "The Making of Metaphor: Another Reading of John 3:1-15," "*What Is John?" Readers and Readings of the Fourth Gospel*, Fernando F. Segovia, ed., Society of Biblical Literature Symposium Series, Gail R. O'Day, ed., no. 3 (Atlanta: Scholars Press, 1996), pp. 21–41.

10. Long (chapter 3) correctly emphasizes that the preacher is the congregation's representative in the interpretative process. As such, we ask the congregation's questions of the text.

11. Cf. Long, chapter 4, for a discussion of focus and function statements.

Chapter 4

1. We borrowed the title of this chapter from the title of a book by Margaret Miles, *Image as Insight: Visual Understanding in Western Christianity and Secular Culture* (Boston: Beacon Press, 1985). On Miles' importance for preaching, cf. Richard L. Eslinger, *Narrative and Imagination: Preaching the Worlds That Shape Us* (Minneapolis: Fortress Press, 1993), pp. 50–57.

2. Cf., for example, David Buttrick, *Homiletic: Moves and Structures* (Philadelphia: Fortress Press, 1987).

3. For a more detailed definition of imagery see Thomas Troeger's article "Figures of Speech" in *Concise Encyclopedia of Preaching*, William H. Willimon and Richard Lischer, eds. (Louisville: Westminster John Knox Press, 1995), p. 139.

4. Patricia Wilson-Kastner expresses the distinction between image and story this way: ". . . narrative is a primary focus for the more temporally conscious mind, imagery a focus for the spatially and visually directed." *Imagery for Preaching*, Fortress Resources for Preaching (Minneapolis: Fortress Press, 1989), p. 21. Cf. Eslinger's proposal for the "intersections" of story and imagery for a more subtle analysis, *Narrative and Imagination*, pp. 70–72.

5. Wilson-Kastner claims simply, "We do in fact think with images" (p. 15).

6. For a brief treatment of the emergence of the prominence of imagination in contemporary homiletics, see Eslinger, pp. 213–23.

7. Cf. Paul Ricoeur, "Paul Ricoeur on Biblical Hermeneutics," *Semeia* 4, John Dominic Crossan, ed. (Missoula, Mont.: Scholars Press, 1975), p. 77, and Sandra M. Schneiders, *The Revelatory Text: Interpreting the New Testament as Sacred Scripture* (New York: HarperCollins, 1991), p. 29.

8. Philip Wheelwright, *Metaphor and Reality* (Bloomington: Indiana University Press, 1962), pp. 72–91. Cf. Sallie McFague, *Speaking in Parables: A Study in Metaphor and Theology* (Philadelphia: Fortress Press, 1975), pp. 106–7.

9. Cf. the classic discussion of symbolism by Paul Tillich, "Religious Symbols and Our Knowledge of God," *The Christian Scholar*, vol. 28, no. 3 (September 1955), pp. 189–97, and *Systematic Theology*, 3 vols. (Chicago: University of Chicago Press, 1951, 1957, 1963), vol. 1, pp. 239–44, and throughout all three of the volumes.

10. Wilson-Kastner, *Imagery for Preaching*, p. 34.

11. Adapted from Erich H. Wahlstrom, *The New Life in Christ* (Philadelphia: Muhlenberg Press, 1950), pp. xvi, 57–86.

12. This sermon is adapted from one preached by Professor Gordon Lathrop of the Lutheran Theological Seminary at Philadelphia for a worship service at a faculty retreat.

13. This sermon is adapted from one preached by Kysar at a chapel service at the Lutheran Theological Seminary at Philadelphia.

14. See the analysis of story in Eugene Lowry, *The Homiletical Plot: The Sermon as Narrative Art Form* (Atlanta: John Knox Press, 1980).

15. For example, Richard A. Jensen, *Thinking in Story: Preaching in a Post-Literate Age* (Lima: C.S.S. Publishing, 1993), pp. 17–66. Cf. chapter 3, "Toward a Theology for Preaching," pp. 67–88.

16. For a fuller discussion of irony, see Eslinger, pp. 117–27.

17. Cf. Richard L. Eslinger, "Narrative and Imagery," *Intersections: Post-Critical Studies in Preaching*, Richard L. Eslinger, ed. (Grand Rapids: Eerdmans 1994), pp. 69–70; Richard Lischer, "The Limits of Story," *Interpretation*, vol. 38, no. 1 (January 1984), pp. 26–38; and *A Theology of Preaching: The Dynamics of the Gospel* (Durham: Labyrinth Press, 1992), for example, pp. 89–90.

18. Richard A. Jensen, *Telling the Story: Variety and Imagination in Preaching* (Minneapolis: Augsburg Publishers, 1980).

19. This is a revision of the conclusion of a sermon Kysar preached at a lay school of theology in western Pennsylvania.

20. For instance, see Richard A. Jensen's helpful discussion of "stitching stories" in *Thinking in Story*, pp. 109–37.

Chapter 5

1. We are indebted to David Buttrick, *Homiletic: Moves and Structures* (Minneapolis: Fortress Press, 1987), pp. 23ff., for taking account of listener attention span in positing three- to four- minute "moves" as building blocks in each sermon. While our research does not confirm many of the details of Buttrick's system, including the length of these formed modules of language, we appreciate his focus on smaller units within the sermon.

2. Gerhard O. Forde, *Theology Is for Proclamation* (Minneapolis: Fortress Press, 1990), p. 39.

3. Fred B. Craddock, *Overhearing the Gospel* (Nashville: Abingdon Press, 1978).

4. We have appreciated the clear linkage of thought and action in Douglas John Hall, *Thinking the Faith: Christian Theology in a North American Context* (Minneapolis: Augsburg Press, 1989), esp. pp. 57–66.

5. David Buttrick, in both *Homiletic* and *The Mystery and the Passion: A Homiletic Reading of the Biblical Traditions* (Minneapolis: Fortress Press, 1992).

6. J. Randall Nichols, *Building the Word: The Dynamics of Communication and Preaching* (New York: Harper and Row, 1980), p. 75. The chapter on "Diagnosis: The Missing Step" is filled with useful insights for preachers who lack diagnostic skills.

7. Bernard J. F. Lonergan, *Insight: A Study of Human Understanding* (New York: Philosophical Library, 1970), p. 9.

8. Paul Tillich, "You Are Accepted," in *A Chorus of Witnesses: Model Sermons for Today's Preacher*, edited by Thomas G. Long and Cornelius Plantinga Jr. (Grand

Rapids: Eerdmans , 1994), p. 99.

9. Neil Postman and Charles Weingartner, *Linguistics: A Revolution in Teaching* (New York: Delacorte Press, 1966), p. 139.

10. Tillich, "You Are Accepted," *A Chorus of Witnesses*, p. 100.

11. Nichols, *Building the Word*, p. 35.

12. Richard S. Worman, *Information Anxiety* (New York: Doubleday, 1989), p. 48.

13. The Rev. Gardner Taylor, at "Preaching Days 90," sponsored by the Philadelphia Chapter of the Academy of Preachers.

14. Buttrick, *Homiletic*, p. 39.

Chapter 6

1. David Buttrick, *Homiletic: Moves and Structures* (Minneapolis: Fortress Press, 1987), p. 310.

2. Professor Nelvin Vos of Muhlenberg College introduced us to the use of viewing instruments as models for various ways of perceiving the world.

3. Harvey Cox, *The Feast of Fools* (New York: Harper and Row, 1969), p. 132.

4. Thomas Long, *Preaching and the Literary Forms of the Bible* (Philadelphia: Fortress Press, 1989), p. 60.

5. Sermon by the Rev. Cindy Ray, Chapel of the Lutheran Theological Seminary at Philadelphia, September 1995.

6. Some of the material in this section appeared in "Sermons Shaped Like Questions," pp. 1–4 in volume 3, no. 2 of *Academy Accents: The Newsletter of the Academy of Preachers.*

7. Douglas John Hall, *Thinking the Faith: Christian Theology in a North American Context* (Minneapolis: Augsburg Press, 1989), p. 85.

8. Ibid., p. 55.

9. John S. McClure, *The Roundtable Pulpit: Where Leadership and Preaching Meet* (Nashville: Abingdon Press, 1995), p. 44.

10. Robert L. Conrad, "Christian Education and Creative Conflict: Relations Between Creative Intrapsychic Conflict as Understood in Luther's Experience and Theology and as Understood in Social Psychological Theories with Conclusions for Christian Education Principles and Practice." Ph.D. dissertation, Princeton Theological Seminary, 1975.

11. Ibid., p. 294.

12. Ibid., p. 295.

13. Ibid., p. 295.

14. H. Grady Davis, *Design for Preaching* (Philadelphia: Fortress Press, 1958).

15. Paul Tillich, *Systematic Theology* (Chicago: University of Chicago Press, 1951, 1957, and 1963, 3 vols.), Vol. I, p. 71.

16. Ibid., Vol. I, p. 72.

17. Herman G. Stuempfle Jr., *Preaching Law and Gospel* (Ramsey, N.J.: Sigler Press, 1990). Originally published by Fortress Press in 1978, this valuable study is once again available in reprint from Sigler with a new introduction. Those desiring to explore the nuances of this sermon model should read the book in full.

18. Ibid., p. 29.

19. Ibid., pp. 54–56.

20. Thomas G. Long, *The Witness of Preaching* (Louisville: Westminster John Knox Press), uses "focus statement" for what the sermon is about and "function statement" for what the preacher hopes will happen for the hearers, p. 86.

21. Walter Brueggemann, *Finally Comes the Poet: Daring Speech for Proclamation* (Minneapolis: Fortress Press, 1989), p. 57.

22. Foster R. McCurley Jr., a former faculty colleague at the Lutheran Theological Seminary at Philadelphia, introduced us to ABBA. It is a pattern prominent in many of his sermons. See *Wrestling with the Word: Christian Preaching from the Hebrew Bible* (Valley Forge, Pa.: Trinity Press International, 1996).

23. Eugene Lowry, *The Homiletical Plot: The Sermon as Narrative Art Form* (Atlanta: John Knox Press, 1980).

24. Brueggemann, p. 109.

Conclusion

1. J. Randall Nichols, *Building the Word: The Dynamics of Communication and Preaching* (New York: Harper and Row, 1980), p. 38.

2. J. Randall Nichols, *The Restoring Word: Preaching as Pastoral Communication* (New York: Harper and Row, 1987), p. 24.

3. Pierre Babin, *The New Era in Religious Communication*, David Smith, trans. (Minneapolis: Fortress Press, 1991), p. 123.

4. Gordon W. Lathrop, *Holy Things: A Liturgical Theology* (Minneapolis: Fortress Press, 1993), p. 51.

5. George A. Miller, "The Magical Number Seven, Plus or Minus Two" in Donald C. Hildum, ed., *Language and Thought* (Princeton, N.J.: D. Van Nostrand, 1967), pp. 3–32, cited in Nichols, *Building the Word*, pp. 52–58.

6. Nichols, *Building the Word*, p. 53.

7. The Rev. Dr. Ernest Campbell, then pastor of Riverside Church in New York City, in a homiletics course taught regularly at Princeton Theological Seminary during the 1970s.

8. "Proactive planning" is a term used by Stephen R. Covey in *The Seven Habits of Highly Effective People* (New York: Simon & Schuster, 1989). While many of the steps described for individuals are easily translated into the corporate/congregational setting, a book more overtly helpful for congregational planning is William M. Easum, *Sacred Cows Make Gourmet Burgers* (Nashville: Abingdon Press, 1995).

9. David Buttrick, *The Mystery and The Passion: A Homiletic Reading of the Biblical Traditions* (Minneapolis: Fortress Press, 1992), pp. 47ff.

10. Ron Crandall, *Turn Around Strategies for the Small Church* (Nashville: Abingdon Press, 1995), pp. 55 and 56.

11. Howard W. Stone and James O. Duke, *How to Think Theologically* (Minneapolis: Fortress Press, 1996), is written to assist laity in reflecting theologically upon key issues. It is suitable for use by adult study groups.

Index of Biblical References

Index of Names and Subjects